OCT 1992

*F*lowers
in
*W*atercolour

Judith Milne.

Flowers in Watercolour

JUDITH MILNE

Judith Milne.

Typeset by Goodfellow & Egan Ltd, Cambridge

and printed in Hong Kong

Published by
B.T. Batsford Ltd
4 Fitzhardinge Street

London W1H 0AH

A catalogue record for this book is available from the British Library

ISBN 0 7134 6403 8

ACKNOWLEDGEMENTS

My sincere and grateful thanks are extended to my family, and many friends who have supported and encouraged me during writing. Special thanks go to my husband, Tony, for his time in typing and checking the script, and my friend Pam Long for her editorial comments. I should also like to thank Daler Rowney for equipment and St Peter's Garden Centre and Palmer's Garden Centre, Worcester for lending me some of their plants.

CONTENTS

Introduction 7

1. A Short History of Flower Painting 10

2. Materials: Paints and Plants 15

3. Drawing 23

4. Colours and Colour Mixing 32

5. Flowers 41

6. Leaves, Stems and Fruits 46

7. Painting in Detail 56

8. Painting Freely 101

9. Framing 125

Index 127

Daisy
Anthemis cupaniana

Judith Milne.

This is a free representation of the daisy. Shadows are used to depict the ridged petals and the yellow centres are worked using small dots of colour. A simple statement such as this can effectively show a plant's character.

INTRODUCTION

Flowers in watercolour – I cannot think of a more exciting subject. I enthuse about all nature, but flowers are very close to my heart. I was brought up in a small village, surrounded by all forms of nature; some of my earliest recollections are walking in the country lanes and watching the first signs of spring: a cluster of primroses nestling in the fresh green foliage, and a carpet of celandines, their bright shiny starlike petals amongst a green bed of leaves. My memories return to the old cottage gardens, and the wealth of colour in the herbaceous borders. It is no different today – we are surrounded by beautiful flowers, and with hundreds of varieties available to us; whether pot plants, garden plants, cut or wild flowers, we never lack subject matter.

   If you are a beginner to flower painting, the question of style is perhaps one of the first things you should address. What way will you paint your subject and what sort of background will you choose? A style of painting is a matter of personal choice, yet for me, flowers are beautiful in their own right and therefore best kept simple. I prefer to work on a white background with the plant in front of me. I never work from photographs but I do take pictures of flowers to show close-up detail and habitat. Painting direct from nature enables me to work in a representational manner – that is, representing the plant as close to life as possible, in terms of colour, shape and character. My paintings are almost always lifesize and so vary from small to large according to the subject. I also like to position my subjects naturally, with as much space around them as possible, so that each plant can be judged on the merits of its own beauty.

   In this book, I intend to explain my way of painting – everyone will have something quite different to contribute but these are the methods I use and the experiences that I have found beneficial. As a teacher, I have always found it imperative to work to a structure, progressing gradually from basic to more complex tasks, and so this

Bearded iris bud. Detail of the painting overleaf.

Bearded iris
Iris pallida

Notice how the deep velvety purple
petals contrast strongly with the
almost translucent yellow petals.
The stem too stands out against the
drying paper-like sheath which
surrounds the bud.

Judith Milne

book is structured in a progressional way, covering a broad spectrum, enabling you to identify a varied amount of subject matter and to tackle most aspects of flower painting. White flowers on white paper, groups of flowerheads, tiny detailed leaf veins or broad, freer-style blooms – whatever your interest, this book will give you a clear insight into a beautiful art.

Detail of the flowerhead.

CHAPTER ONE

A SHORT HISTORY OF FLOWER PAINTING

It is possible to trace botanical art back to the earliest civilizations. Plants and flowers feature crudely in Egyptian art; stone-relief carvings at the Great Temple at Karnak dating from 1450 BC show simple, stylized representations of plants. Yet it was not until plants were appreciated for their medicinal value that they featured prominently in art. During the Renaissance, plants and flowers were painted more precisely and realistically than ever before by artists such as Durer and Da Vinci. Woodcuts heralded the beginnings of fine reproductions, and Brunfel's *Herbanum Vivae Eicones*, published in 1530, was the start of scientific illustration. Gradually, line engravings and etchings on metal took over from woodcuts, and the lines became even finer and more precise.

Besides precise scientific records of flowers in engravings, flowers in oil were also very popular, particularly in the Netherlands in the fifteenth and sixteenth centuries. The Flemish and Dutch painters rarely made their pictures direct from nature, but composed them from studies and drawings; often flowers from several seasons were incorporated in one painting. Besides acting as vehicles for displays of the painter's skill, these paintings also had an unusual commercial value. *The Tulip Books*, as they were called, were in fact sale catalogues, commissioned by bulb dealers so that they could sell their flowers when out of season.

Interest in botanical illustration grew as artists travelled more widely and more plants were introduced from abroad. The eighteenth century produced many examples of quality flower painting, and Britain was at the forefront of this development. Georg Dionysius Ehret (1708–70) was the main influence in botanical painting. Born in Germany, he painted with body colour on vellum – a technique which he preferred to paper and transparent wash, and being a great draughtsman, he captured the finest detail in even the smallest drawing. Dionysius moved to England in 1736 and found great patronage there, painting right up until the time of his death.

Les Liliacées No. 10 by Pierre Joseph
Redouté.

Another great painter was the Belgian artist Joseph Redouté (1759–1840) who moved to France to work with his brother, where he painted stage scenery to earn his living. Under the tutelage of a wealthy botanist at the *Jardin du Roi*, he published his own floral studies as engravings. Redouté's pure watercolour, finely gradated with touches of body colour for highlights, soon became his trademark, and his following of devotees included Marie Antoinette and Josephine Bonaparte.

Meanwhile in Britain, the publication of *The Botanical Magazine* in 1787 by William Curtis was testimony to the ever-increasing interest in floral art. Curtis, a London apothecary, understood his patrons' desires for a magazine depicting bright garden flowers, and supervised a team of engravers to begin such work. William Kilburn, James Sowerby and Sydenham Edwards were among the long-standing artists employed by Curtis. Eventually, William

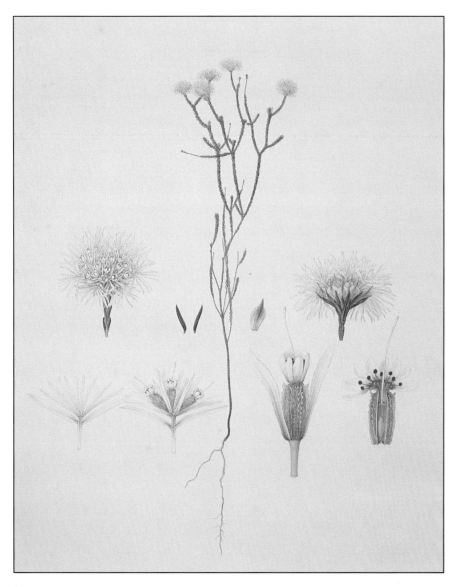

Actinodium Cunninghari by Ferdinand Bauer (*left*).

Agapanthus by Walter Hood Fitch (*right*).

Hooker took over the magazine before becoming the Director of Kew Gardens. The association with Kew ensured that *The Botanical Magazine* was acknowledged for its high quality and accurate botanical illustrations, and until 1948 every plate was still coloured by hand. Today the magazine is produced quarterly.

Other botanical artists, such as the German Ferdinand Bauer (1760–1826) and Walter Hood Fitch (1817–92), maintained the traditions of botanical painting over the centuries, but in the nineteenth century scientific flower work became the domain of women. As such, it was regarded as a genteel pastime for ladies, who devoted much time to careful analyses of the local flora and fauna. Edith Holden's beautiful nature diary, and the four cousins whose work is now published as a book called *The Frampton Flora*, are some of the most recently admired artists who were sadly never discovered in their own lifetimes. Women artists became more prominent, however, at the beginning of the twentieth century – Lilian Snelling was the principal artist of *The Botanical Magazine*, followed by Stella Ross-Craig, Mary Grierson, Pandora Sellers and Margaret Stones of the present day.

If you are interested in any of these artists, much of their work can still be seen in botanical museums. To start with, try visiting the Natural History Museum, the Herbarium at Kew and the Lindley Library of the Royal Horticultural Society.

CHAPTER TWO

MATERIALS: PAINTS AND PLANTS

Never before have we had such a vast variety of materials from which to choose; the art shop can be completely confusing for any newcomer, with its ever-changing stock. But don't overload yourself with equipment – in fact it is better to seek the advice of friends and perhaps even try out their own equipment before you invest in any. Always buy the best though, when you are confident with what you want.

PAINTS

When I first started to paint, I worked with students' colours; after a little while I changed to artists' colours. The difference in quality was amazing and my whole attitude to my work changed. Magically, it took on a new depth and vibrancy and my paintings were much more satisfying. Now I only use artists' watercolours and although they seem expensive initially, they do last a long time.

A box of pans, pencils, brushes and a carrying box (*above*).

A selection of brushes, tubes and a box of pans (*right*).

Students are surprised to see me using a box of half-pans rather than tubes of watercolours. I find these especially good when working on a small painting. I use tubes if I am working on large scale pictures, however, and use a large covered palette where I can squeeze out my paints, and cover them up until the next time I need them. These palettes are approximately 30 × 20cm (12 × 8in) and contain two large areas for mixing – base and top; when the cover is put over the base, any residue of paint is protected from dust and is easily transported. The wells of the paintbox palette are quite sufficient for mixing when using pans. The basic set of colours does not always provide a wide enough range for flower painting, so I add more half-pans to the brush-well of the box, giving me a further eleven or twelve half-pans, and thus providing me with a total of thirty-seven colours. As the paint does not wear evenly, I find it very convenient to fill worn pans with pigment from tubes, rather than replace them with new pans, as this avoids wastage of paint. I also find it very useful to keep a sketching box of eighteen quarter-pans of artists' colours in my car, so I always have equipment with me.

NB: Never wash the dried paint from tubes off your palette, as this will dry and can be used like a pan. Even a dried up tube can be slit open and used in the same way!

Gouache can also be classed as watercolour, because these paints are dissolved in water. However, they are opaque rather than translucent, and when used produce a chalky effect – although this can be effective. Gouache paint was introduced for designers who needed broad flat areas of paint, but they are used widely for all painting subjects, including flowers. If needing a particularly brilliant hue, I do use some in the gouache range to mix with the watercolours, although I generally prefer to use watercolour, as the quality of the paint lends itself to the delicate translucency of most plants.

Coloured inks are used by some artists to supplement watercolour, or on their own to create an image; the same colour range can be obtained for these as for gouache and watercolour, but they give a glazed appearance and their colour is not always permanent. Paints also need to be cared for. Do not leave palettes and paintboxes uncovered, as dust and animal hairs in the atmosphere will settle on them, so giving a rough surface to your paint.

PENCILS

Pencils are a basic requirement, essential for preparatory drawings. Fairly fine drawing is necessary for plant study, so I always recommend using nothing softer than a B (2B, 3B, 4B, 5B and 6B are more suitable for general sketching). HB (middle of the range in thickness) is the most suitable for most plant drawing. H and 2H can be used for very fine work, but pressed too hard cut into the paper leaving marks which cannot be erased. More often than not I use an F, which is middle of the range between H and HB; it can be used for most types of work, keeps a fine point, and does not easily smudge. Always use a pencil of good length, as it is more comfortable to handle.

A soft eraser is a must, otherwise the surface of the paper becomes damaged and unsuitable for painting. I use a putty eraser most of the time as it is soft and easily lifts out marks, without needing pressure or causing the paper damage. A putty eraser is malleable, and therefore can be moulded into shape to erase between narrow lines and in corners, and can also be used to create highlights in a shaded area.

Do use a fixative on all pencil drawings that you want to keep, to protect them from smudging. This applies particularly where softer pencils are used, but fixative should *not* be used when you are going to paint on a drawing.

Water-soluble pencils are not essential, but a useful medium for outdoor note-making, and more complex studies. It is not essential for them to be used with a wash of clear water, but this gives them another dimension. They can be bought individually or in boxed sets. The colours do mix, so it is a good idea to have a wide variety of colours if you want to use them in a full-scale painting. Water-soluble pencils can be used with pen and ink to give a wash effect.

PEN AND INK

In the chapter on drawing (see page 23), I refer to the use of pen and ink. The cheapest materials are a mapping pen and Indian ink for general pen and ink drawing, but the flexibility of the nib can cause the width of the line to vary. More satisfactory is a designer's pen, which gives a constant flow of ink and a line of consistent thickness, ideal for botanical art. The nibs vary in thickness although the finest one is most suitable.

MASKING MEDIUM

This is a resist to paint and is a useful asset, but not essential. Apply the fluid with an old brush (never use a new brush as the rubber solution will clog the hairs) to areas which need to be left white whilst you paint surrounding detail. The medium can then be peeled off to reveal the desired shape beneath. I find it particularly useful for keeping stamens very light against darker petals in a broad wash, but I don't use it frequently.

PAPER

The choice of watercolour paper is a very personal one, the right one only being found by trial and error. Cartridge paper, either in sheets or pads, is fine for sketching and note-taking, but inappropriate for a finished painting. Nothing is more frustrating than to have the paper cockle under your wash of paint and lose its even surface, so it is as well to buy watercolour paper from the start. Bear in mind that it is expensive for experimentation, so reserve it for what you intend to be a completed piece of work.

The best watercolour papers are hand-made, produced in practically the same way as they were centuries ago. They are expensive, but there is also a wide variety of cheaper papers, which are very good substitutes.

Watercolour paper must accept colour accurately and fast, and also withstand repeated washes of colour. The best papers are acid-free. These accurately represent the artist's palette and do not discolour. Paper comes in pads of varying sizes and sheets can usually be purchased in different weights from 90lb (190 gsm), the lightest, through 140lb (300 gsm), 200lb (425 gsm) and 300lb (640 gsm), to 400lb (850 gsm), which is the heaviest. The most popular weight is 140lb (300 gsm), a good firm paper, very suitable for flower painting, where large washes are not used. The heavier papers are useful for larger paintings where you need to use broad washes.

Stretching paper is one precaution against wrinkling but it may not be necessary for small-scale work. To stretch paper, wet the paper on both sides and place it on a drawing board. Then stick it to the board with wet gummed tape, running it around all edges of the paper, partly on the paper and the board. Initially the paper will be rumpled, but will dry taut and will return to this state even after a number of washes. If you use 90lb (190 gsm), I would recommend stretching if its size is 28 × 38cm (11 × 15in) or more. However, I mainly use 140lb (300 gsm) paper and, unless I need a background wash, work quite happily to half imperial size without stretching.

The surface of the paper is an important consideration. The three surfaces obtainable are Rough, Not and Hot-Pressed (HP). Your choice depends on your requirements. The Rough surface, as its name implies, is coarse, with wells in the paper holding the colour. This is really more suitable for broad landscape painting. The Not surface ('Not' meaning 'not Hot-Pressed') is the middle of the range, having an even texture with a good 'tooth' to it. The Hot-Pressed is the smoothest paper and is particularly suitable for very fine painting, but I also use Not when I am working in a freer style. Pads and blocks of paper can usually be obtained in Not and sometimes in Rough, but the HP can only be found in the large sheets. This is not a problem, as it is possible to cut it up to the required sizes. In addition, there are watercolour boards that can be obtained in all three surfaces. Experiment and discover for yourself what suits you. The choice is very personal as types of paper not only vary in surface, but in absorbency too. There are tinted papers designed for watercolour, and pastel papers. Be careful with pastel paper, however, as it is flimsy and cockles easily; always mount it on board before use, and reserve it for gouache or thick watercolour.

Protect your paper when working at all times by using a piece of kitchen roll or another clean sheet of paper under your hand. Paper will absorb grease and dust from your hands, and cause you problems when applying washes.

You may be able to afford a drawing board, a base for your work, or improvise with hardboard pieces or plywood offcuts. In any case, ensure that the surface is smooth under the paper.

BRUSHES

Brushes are an expensive commodity, so should always be chosen carefully. Again a good quality tool is much better to work with, so spend as much as you can afford. The quality of the hair is a very important factor, as well as the point, which produces the perfect shape. The choice of brushes is enormous, so seek advice at a local art shop. The pure red sable, the best brush for watercolour, is very expensive, but if treated with care it will last a long time. Sable absorbs and retains liquid, unlike synthetic brushes, but the latter are very good substitutes and much cheaper. I use sable and

A variety of brushes was used in this free painting. For broad washes of colour I used a No. 6, but I then changed to a No. 3 for smaller areas. The fine veining on the pink was worked with a No. 1 rigger; I added the fine hairs with a size 00 brush.

Petunias

synthetic brushes; the latter I find are excellent and last reasonably well. When the point goes, you will have to discard the brush, but you can use it for applying masking fluid, or working with acrylics or a thicker medium. Other cheaper varieties of brush are oxhair, or a mixture of sable and oxhair; they hold water well, but do not have a fine point, or the springiness of a sable brush. There is also a mixture of sable and synthetic, which has the character of a sable brush, but the nylon makes it more durable.

Sizes range from the large size 20 to the very fine 00000, and your choice depends on the type and size of your work. I find numbers 10, 8 or 6 useful for applying washes; I then always keep a selection of the sizes down to No 1, and a number of the very fine ones, which are ideal for detailed centres and veining. After the initial wash, I seldom use anything larger than a No 2, and then build up fine work with No 1.0 or 000. *Flat* or *bright* brushes are also useful as their chisel edge can be run in a straight line. The *rigger*, with its long flexible hairs, is good for detail, and any flicking movements such as the application of fine lines for veining, but it is not possible to maintain the control you have with the shorter-haired, round brushes.

Always buy brushes with a good point. You can check the quality of your brush by dipping it into a pot of water and shaking it – the brush should have a smooth shape when wet. To keep your brush in good condition, store it in a plastic cover and never leave it in water. Bending will also damage your brush irretrievably.

OTHER MATERIALS

Dividers are a very useful asset when measuring the size of a plant, and a magnifying glass is a must for observing the detail of tiny flowers or the centres of flowers. A hand-held one is sufficient, but one on a stand allows more freedom to observe and draw. It is a good idea to store all your work and monitor your progress. Sketch books are compact, but odd pieces of paper with reference notes are easily lost, so keep them together in a folder. Keep any unframed pictures in a folder in a dry place and away from direct sunlight; for special protection you can even attach tissue or greaseproof paper to each painting.

PLANT MATERIAL

Plants are your subject matter, but you also need to understand and care for them, like any other of your working tools. The life duration of a plant, once picked, varies considerably; some wilt soon after picking, and climatic conditions can also affect their lives. Where possible, put picked specimens into water at once; very small, delicate plants are most vulnerable and wilt easily. While working, it may be necessary to hold the plant for close inspection; keep it in water if possible, or return it immediately after examination. For small, individual plants a retort stand holding a test tube of water is

This beautiful blossom was created using a stippling technique with fine brushes.

Tamarisk
Tamarix

a good idea, as it is possible to adjust the plant's position without taking it out of the water. For more robust, perhaps woody-stemmed, varieties, the plant can be clipped on the stand and its stem set into wet cottonwool or floral foam. A container of floral foam will also hold your plant firm and allow you to position it in a variety of angles. If you know your flower will only live a short time, and perhaps not sufficiently long enough to complete the painting, ensure that there are buds which will open to succeed it.

Changes in temperature will alter the plant's shape rapidly: petals will curl and twist in a short time, and leaves will droop, so never work in intense heat or direct sunlight if you can avoid it. In a long hot summer, conditions can be difficult and very frustrating, as not only do plants fade quickly, but paint dries rapidly too, so washes are problematic and your palette is constantly dry. To maintain a rose in bud, put it in the refrigerator; this holds it in that position, but subsequently the rose will not become full-blown.

Some woody-stemmed plants retain their own moisture for some time, but others, like magnolia, do not respond well to cutting and virtually change in front of your eyes. Yet it is possible to paint *in situ*, where you are able to study growth patterns and compare with other flowers of the same variety, but this has its problems too. We seldom have days that are absolutely still, and it is impossible to study closely when your specimen is wafting in the breeze.

Pot plants, for durability, are probably the easiest to work from, although their size can be daunting, but it is not essential to paint the whole plant. Spring flowers hold a particular appeal for me, so in the autumn I plant lots of bulbs in pots, leave them to grow naturally out-of-doors, and when in bloom, I bring them in for working. Another alternative is to dig up a garden plant, with plenty of soil, put it into a large container, and then work in suitable conditions. I hasten to add that this should not be done with wild plants, as there is sufficient depletion already in the countryside, and it is in fact illegal to pick them.

When choosing your plant, whether from the garden, or from a florist, check to see that it is good quality, that flowers and leaves are not badly damaged, that there are plenty of buds too, and that flowers are not all full-blown before starting drawing or painting. I do not mean that the plant should be absolutely perfect in condition, as it is more realistic and interesting to represent true markings, such as certain discolourations or holes where a caterpillar has feasted! Look also at the shape of the plant; choose one which lends itself to the image you want to make. Do not choose something that is badly formed, but go for a stem or branch which displays its flowers to good advantage, and makes a pleasant design on your page, without needing manipulation.

CHAPTER THREE

DRAWING

A body is useless without its skeletal framework. For a painting the drawing is that framework, a base on which to build – a painting is only as good as the drawing underneath it. If that foundation is good and strong, then what follows should also be good. With shape, form, tone and colour sense combined, the end result will be a structured image. Even in a painting where no pencil or outline is used, that ability to draw, to set out an image, to make the eye understand the total concept, is the key to successful painting.

Many students decide to take up painting, set off to the local art shop, and buy all the necessary paints and brushes without really thinking about the drawing techniques required. One has only to recall the work of the old masters, and the folios of sketches and drawings they made before a piece of work was begun: why should we lesser mortals feel that we can launch into a painting without preparation?

Preparation may seem laborious, when all you want to do is paint a masterpiece. However, if you adopt the attitude that anything you produce is a contribution to the perfection of that end result, the preparation can be exciting and rewarding in itself, and all aspects of it, whether drawing, sketching or colour or technical experiments, can all be shown as part of the learning process.

It is not important to have a lot of equipment for drawing; see the previous chapter for suggestions. You just need a few sketchbooks, a small one for keeping in a pocket or bag, and a medium-to-large one depending on the scale of your work, of reasonable quality cartridge paper. Keep your sketchbooks, and date each piece of work. There is nothing better for boosting the deflated ego than to look back on previous work and note gradual progress.

Sketches are also important for information – make your drawings quick and numerous, showing your object from different angles, and refer to them often for reference information.

As a basis for painting, a linear drawing is perfectly adequate –

Leopard's bane
Doronicum

Judith Milne.

Cape leadwort
Plumbago auriculata

that is, a map showing your composition, and an outline of the subject to be painted. However, in the case of flower painting, more detailed preparatory exercises are helpful. Owing to the delicacy of the subject matter, it is best to make clear, simple studies, using an HB, F or H pencil. Always make your lines faint in the first instance, as heavy lines may press into the surface of the paper and cannot be erased. For a painting you only require faint outlines as a guide, so whether you are drawing an outline for painting or a drawn study, you begin in the same way.

Deciding on composition is the first priority when preparing a painting, so look at your subject matter, decide on how you want your finished image to look, and at this stage make a number of thumbnail sketches, showing different positions, and choose the most suitable. A single daisy or a rose will not look natural if positioned centrally, so place it at a slight angle across your page. It may be necessary to add extra leaves, or another flower to improve on the composition.

I added more detailed drawings to this quick sketch for reference (*left*).

Study sheets showing detailed sections of plants (*right*).

Yellow wort
Blackstonia perfoliata

A PREPARATORY SKETCH FOR A PAINTING

Having chosen your composition, now begin your drawing study. Your paper should be slightly larger than your finished piece of work. Allow a margin for notes, experiments with colour and mounting. Make your first marks directional, like the laying of a map, and faint. Indicate the direction of the stem and the position and angle of the flowerhead. Within that head, as in the example of the rose on page 29, the petals vary in direction too, so look carefully at this. Make sure the centre does not protrude to a point, but sits neatly around the seed box. This is where understanding the formation of a flower can be so helpful. Size is another important factor; use your pencil and thumb for measuring, so that you can compare lengths and widths vertically and horizontally, to ensure correct proportion.

It is important to depict the angles at which the leaves come off the stem and the direction they follow for an accurate three-dimensional effect, but a simple line following the shape and direction is sufficient at this stage. As long as your lines are light, you can easily make alterations later. Now you have your basic foundation for a painting.

A LINEAR STUDY

A linear drawing is the next stage, as in the example of the autumn leaf shown on page 28. Make a simple outline of the subject; erase or work over the rough guidelines, and you have in front of you a drawing ready, either for detailed drawing and shading, or for painting. It is advisable to have a good point on your pencil, although not too sharp, and lines should still not need to be hard or incised into the paper. You may find that you 'worry' at your line instead of making it clear and direct, and thus end up with a hazy outline. In landscape drawing or sketching this is more acceptable, but the delicacy and fineness of plant subject matter requires a different approach. With careful study and practice, you will be

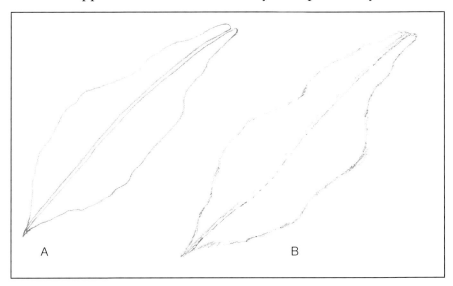

A is a controlled line drawing, whereas B has a 'feathery' appearance which is not so suitable for precise flower painting.

Cow parsley (Queen Anne's lace)
Anthriscus sylvestris

A detailed study worked actual
size, showing a hairy, ridged stem
and a multiple flowerhead.

able to memorize the shapes and patterns you see in front of you, and transmit those as a controlled line. It is also important to convey the shapes *between* the objects you are drawing. Look for the shapes that occur between petals, leaves, etc. and by combining them with the shape of the petal or leaf you are drawing, you will achieve a more accurate interpretation. An interesting exercise is to make a drawing using just the in-between shapes; correctly observed, the result will be the 'negative' version of the 'positive' drawing.

With your linear drawing as a base, you can proceed to paint or develop the drawing as a study.

A TONAL STUDY

Now, with the addition of tone, it is possible to achieve a three-dimensional effect. Tone, the variation of depth of colour, showing the light and shade, immediately alters the image of a linear drawing. The degree of tone expressed is dependent on the contrast of light, and the play of light on varying plains or surfaces.

In the case of the rose, I used an F pencil throughout, varying the degree of tone by gently building up pencil marks until I obtained the necessary depth. Make sure that the pressure exerted on the pencil is light, so that no hard edges are shown. Petals usually curve gently, and this can be shown by grading the pencil line so that the pencil fades into the lightest area. Always make sure that the lines of your shading follow the growth pattern and curves of the leaf or petal you draw. Never work across those lines. Certain areas between petals will be in very deep shadow, as will the edge of a petal as it curves away from the centre of the plant.

Do not labour the shading, as it is ever important to convey the delicacy of petals, but work the pencil softly backwards and forwards over the surface of the paper to build up a layer of tone gradually. Do not use your finger to smudge your pencil marks, as this leads to a burnished effect that is only suitable for metal objects. The shiny stem of the rose will have very definite highlights along it, but these will vary according to the shape and curve of the plant and will not necessarily appear along its entire length. In a drawing like this it is not possible to delineate every vein on every petal and leaf, as the confusion of lines will destroy the image. With half-closed eyes you can determine the definite shaded areas, putting in the shade that is best going to describe your image.

On the other hand, look at the finished drawing of a curled leaf. Where the underside of the leaf curls round, it shows the pronounced veins, which add a certain amount of interest, and because of their protrusion, are accentuated by shadows. Note how the shading on the curled leaf follows the curve and disappears into the lightest area.

The above studies show a clear linear drawing of an autumn leaf. The completed detailed study is worked tonally. It creates texture and a three dimensional feeling.

These lines are the first marks I make at the start of a drawing. They show the varying directions and angles.

Rose
Rosa

This finished drawing shows the different tones and shapes of the flower, leaves and stem. I completed this one hour after sketching the first few guidelines.

Rubber plant (India rubber tree)
Ficus elastica

This detailed drawing shows the all-important joints between the leaf stalk and the main stem.

Rose hip

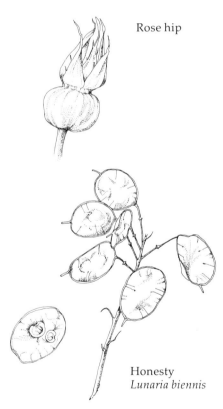

Honesty
Lunaria biennis

Pen and ink studies showing tone and fine details. It is possible, at this stage, to add colour washes using thin layers of watercolour.

Emphasis of line can give depth to a drawing without tone. For this, first decide on the importance of a line. For example, the edge of a leaf or petal nearest to you can be strengthened, while the one furthest away from you remains faint, and so the lines are graded from the front to the back of the object. Single directional lines of form, such as in a curling petal, will denote roundness.

The drawing on the left of the India rubber tree (*Ficus elastica*) shows the importance of structure, and the point of growth. The leaf and stem joints are very important details: study them both in drawing and painting. The fleshy leaves and stems of the rubber plant show clearly how the stem, leaf stem and vein are formed. Experimental, working drawings like this are valuable reference material.

A brief word on the use of pen and ink. This method of drawing is used widely in botanical illustration, and can be very satisfying. The rose hip and honesty (*Lunaria biennis*) were worked first in pencil, to the linear stage. Use a designer's pen for this: here I used a 0.35 nib to draw the outline. To indicate the shading, you can use any of several methods: either stipple or dot, lines following contour, hatching or straight lines. I prefer the effect of stipple, which I have used here, letting the stipple follow the shape and forming the tone (concentration creates a deeper tone). On a large plant stippling is very time-consuming, but nevertheless very effective.

Water-soluble crayons are a useful medium, both for quick studies and fine drawings. I worked with these in a free way, with no base drawing, but using the crayons as a pencil. The range of colours is good, but there is not quite the flexibility of watercolour. Since the colours mix it is possible to layer them to obtain effective contrasts. Each colour can be used as light or as dark as pressure dictates, giving a greater variety to the colours available. For fine detail make sure that the point is well sharpened. Crayon is impossible to erase, so be sure of the mark you make. Here I worked the middle of the centre first, beginning with the lightest shade and progressing to the deepest. I drew in the lightest mauve of the petals, subsequently emphasizing the ridging, either with more pressure or a darker shade. The greens are not quite appropriate, but with a combination of several, and also yellow and blue, it is possible to make a more accurate colour. Always work from the palest shades through to the darkest, finally emphasizing tone, and in conclusion, as in any painting or drawing, accentuate the tones to give a good balance of contrast.

Here I show the effective use of water-soluble crayons in the painting process.

Michaelmas daisy
Aster novi-belgii

Judith Milne.

CHAPTER FOUR

COLOURS AND
COLOUR MIXING

Note the lighter and darker shades of colour which can be seen in both the bracts and the leaves (*right*).

The detail below of the flower and leaves shows the range of colours used.

Understanding colour, and the art of colour mixing, are important in any form of painting and design, but when you are working in a representational way, as in flower painting, those skills are essential.

With experience gained by using colour constantly, it is possible to look at a petal or leaf and immediately analyse the component parts which should be mixed to achieve the desired colour. It is seldom feasible to use a colour directly from your paintbox though; the variety of colours and hues in plants is so vast that you need to mix as many permutations as you can. Gather a random selection of

Poinsettia
Euphorbia pulcherrima

A good example of variety of colour. The colours in the bloom range from blues through mauves to pink and I used different depths of shadow for the 'pleated' petals. For the pale green leaves, I used Lemon Yellow and Sap Green, while a mixture of Sage Green and French Ultramarine was ideal for the shadows and hollows. I worked the noduled stem in a variety of colours, the lightest being pale Raw Sienna, with Raw Umber and French Ultramarine added in degrees to obtain different tones. The centres of the nodules show touches of green.

Hibiscus
H. syriacus 'Blue Bird'

leaves from plants in your garden and then lay them on a sheet of paper. The variety of greens before you is amazing; not only will their basic colour be very different, but their tones will add yet more variation to that range.

Watercolour paints are made from finely ground pigments mixed with gum arabic. The quality of the paint is determined by the ingredients, which is why colours are coded according to their price category: for example, real Ultramarine is made from pure ground lapis lazuli, and is therefore expensive, whereas more readily found pigments are cheaper. Artists' watercolour paints are finely ground and of the highest quality, and do not contain as many additives as students' paints.

Watercolour is a transparent medium, ideal for a luminous effect, but there are some colours which do not have that quality and are noted as semi-transparent. Permanence of colour is given a star rating by manufacturers, who denote those that have the highest degree of fastness to light and those that are inert to other pigments. The least permanent watercolours are known as 'fugitive', and you should avoid using them as they will fade.

In pure watercolour technique, you use the white of the paper to form the lightest part of a painting. For dark shades lay thin washes of colour over one another until the desired effect is achieved, always working through from the lightest shade to the darkest. With watercolour, once the statement is made there is generally no going back – you cannot lighten something once you have applied your colour – so think carefully before applying each layer. There are times when it is possible to lift some colour with clear water and a tissue or clean brush, but more often than not, staining remains.

It may sometimes be necessary to add body colour. Take, for example, instances of hairs on a dark leaf, as in the African violet (*Saint paulia*) on page 51, where I used opaque colour. How much body colour you use is a matter of personal choice.

On page 16 I mentioned that because of the accuracy of colour I wanted to achieve in flower painting, it was essential to supplement the range of colours in my paintbox. Conversely, there are always one or two colours that are superfluous to requirements. I very rarely use black, but prefer to mix my own dark shades, as one never sees a true black in flowers. The black colours tend to lean towards purple, blue or brown.

The chart on page 36 shows the colours I use most. A good choice of yellows and blues is important as the basis for mixing a wide variety of greens, to add to the existing greens in my palette. I do not use Viridian on its own, but it can occasionally be useful mixed with another colour. Prussian Blue is also a very strong colour and needs to be used in moderation. Naples Yellow is rather opaque but mixed with Permanent Red it turned out to be right for peach-coloured gladioli (see page 70).

Here I show the variety of colour-depth you can obtain by adding varying amounts of water to your pigment.

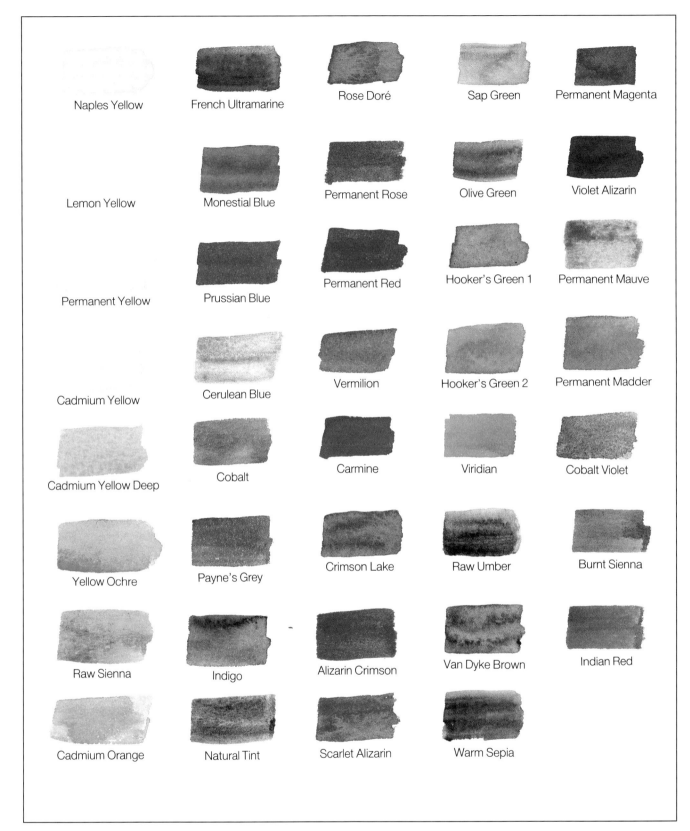

Naples Yellow	French Ultramarine	Rose Doré	Sap Green	Permanent Magenta
Lemon Yellow	Monestial Blue	Permanent Rose	Olive Green	Violet Alizarin
Permanent Yellow	Prussian Blue	Permanent Red	Hooker's Green 1	Permanent Mauve
Cadmium Yellow	Cerulean Blue	Vermilion	Hooker's Green 2	Permanent Madder
Cadmium Yellow Deep	Cobalt	Carmine	Viridian	Cobalt Violet
Yellow Ochre	Payne's Grey	Crimson Lake	Raw Umber	Burnt Sienna
Raw Sienna	Indigo	Alizarin Crimson	Van Dyke Brown	Indian Red
Cadmium Orange	Natural Tint	Scarlet Alizarin	Warm Sepia	

The range of colour I use in my box
of pans.

So many flowers come within the pink range that it is useful to include a wide variety of reds and pinks, so here I added Rose Doré, Carmine, Crimson Lake and Scarlet Alizarin. Permanent Magenta, Permanent Mauve and Cobalt Violet also come into their own for rich hues. Payne's Grey, Indigo and Natural Tint are good for shading, but use them in small amounts and be careful to get the combination right: avoid making shadows too blue. It is always worth experimenting with any colour mix first.

When you have selected your paints, test their quality by beginning with neat colour and diluting by degrees to see what variety of tone is possible. Understanding your tools is very important. Become acquainted with each colour, and know whether it is transparent or semi-transparent; generally play with them and experience the excitement of obtaining a mix that you did not think was possible. Remember that the colour you apply to your paper will be lighter when it is dry, but you will soon learn how much to apply.

In order to appreciate fully the colours of your box, make yourself a labelled reference chart and then make mixture charts like the ones illustrated here and on pages 38 and 39. Take all your yellows and blues and mix each blue with each yellow in turn, and see the permutations you can obtain. Each of those in their turn can vary with the amount of blue or yellow, so giving you an even wider choice. Always label your colours, as charts such as these are invaluable reference material which you can turn to over and over again. It means that at a glance you can see the colour you desire, and know immediately how to create it.

You will notice that some combinations, for example, Permanent Rose and French Ultramarine, or Cobalt and Monestial Blue, give a much clearer mauve/purple than others (see page 39), though murkier shades may be very useful for certain plants such as orchids!

In the case of the reds/oranges, you can see that out of nine colours it is possible to mix a further twenty, so giving a good range of oranges through to browns. These are based on the mix of 50:50, but 25:75, with the emphasis on either yellow or red, will give an even greater variation. The range can be further extended by adding water as the chart shows.

When painting flowers you must avoid that muddy colour which will result if you do not keep your brushes and palette clean. Before embarking on a painting, always ensure that your palette is clean. True colour should always be your aim, and the wrong shade can indicate another variety of plant. Your flower will probably not be the same colour throughout; it may shade to a paler or darker centre, which means grading your wash for the paler shade by adding more water to dilute the density of the colour. If you are

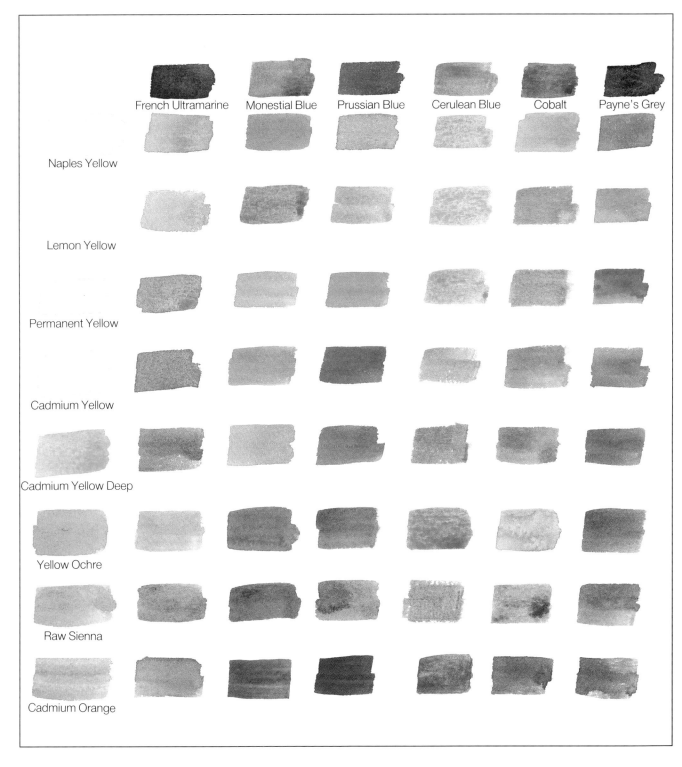

French Ultramarine Monestial Blue Prussian Blue Cerulean Blue Cobalt Payne's Grey

Naples Yellow

Lemon Yellow

Permanent Yellow

Cadmium Yellow

Cadmium Yellow Deep

Yellow Ochre

Raw Sienna

Cadmium Orange

The chart on the left shows the wide variety of greens you can obtain by mixing different blues and yellows.

The chart on this page shows the variety of oranges and purples you can obtain by experimental mixing.

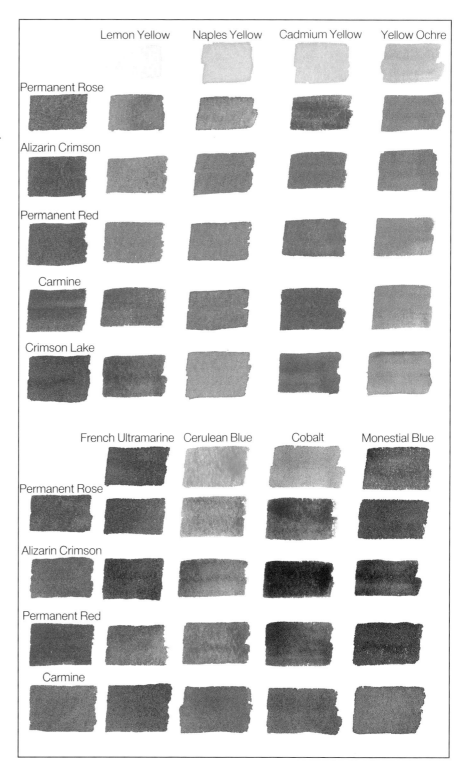

blending in additional colours, they must be introduced while the paint is still damp, so avoiding harsh lines. Look at the gladioli on page 70.

Although it is wise to keep your palette clean, sometimes it is useful to keep your mixture of greens from a previous painting. They may prove to be just the right colour for some small patch you are painting, and it avoids extra mixing. I always try to keep my greens mixed on a separate area of palette, away from the flower colour.

The nature of flower painting is such that you will usually be working on a fairly small area, but you must still apply your first washes evenly. Many students make the mistake of not mixing sufficient colour, and therefore find it difficult to match a succeeding mix. Allow your brush to take up plenty of paint, using a suitably sized brush for the area you are working on. Lay the wash evenly over the shape, keeping the paint fluid and moving constantly until you have covered the entire area. Dried, hard lines will spoil the effect, and they are difficult to remove. For larger areas dampen the paper first with clear water, so that the colour flows over the surface evenly. Never apply the paint so thickly that the paper is obliterated, and the quality of watercolour is lost. Painting dry colour is a superficial process to add a surface texture or effect, and is applied over laid translucent washes.

CHAPTER FIVE

FLOWERS

It is very important to understand the structure of a flower before you even begin to paint it, so I suggest you first dissect a flowerhead to see how it all fits together. The usual example of the perfect flower is the buttercup, shown overleaf in section.

Each flowerhead or bud is protected by a group of greenish leaves called sepals, or the calyx; the next group of leaves is the petals, which vary in colour according to type and species. In many flowering plants, the leaves occur in definite numbers, for example, four sepals, four petals and four or eight stamens. Of course, there are exceptions. Some petals and sepals remain separate, but other plants, such as the foxglove (*Digitalis*), are tubular, as the petals have fused for virtually the whole length of the flowerhead. There are other irregular flowers, like the white deadnettle (*Lamium album*), which has five fused petals, but under-developed lower petals. The lupin (*Lupinus*) is another irregular flower, its five petals not all joined but of different shapes and sizes. Two of the petals are partly fused to form protection round the stamens and ovary. Meanwhile the composites – such as dandelions (*Taraxacum officinale*) – appear to have many petals, but they actually comprise many single florets or flowerheads. Each flowerhead consists of petals, stamens, stigma and ovary.

The name given to the arrangement of flowers on a stem or branch is an *inflorescence*. Besides the composite inflorescence there is a *raceme*, which is unbranched with flowers borne at equal distances along the stem on flower stalks of equal length. An example of this is the English bluebell or wild hyacinth (*Hyacinthoides non-scripta*). The *spike* is an inflorescence in which the flowers, without a stalk, occur round an axis. An example of this is the hyacinth (*Hyacinthus*). The tulip is an example of a single flower.

The *umbel* is a flowerhead with equal leaf stalks proceeding from the central stem, for example flowering rush (*Butomus umbellatus*),

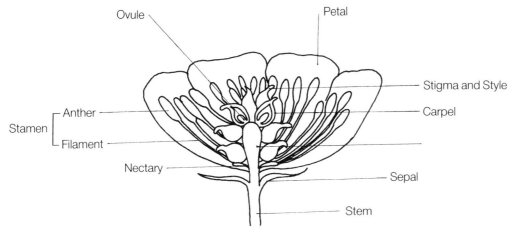

a. Section of buttercup.

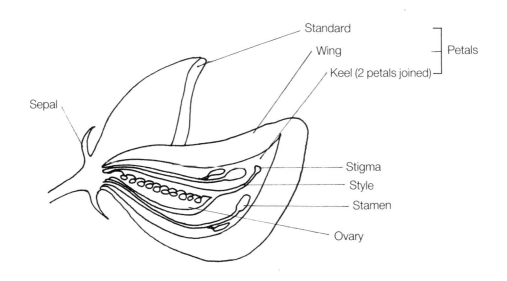

b. Section of lupin.

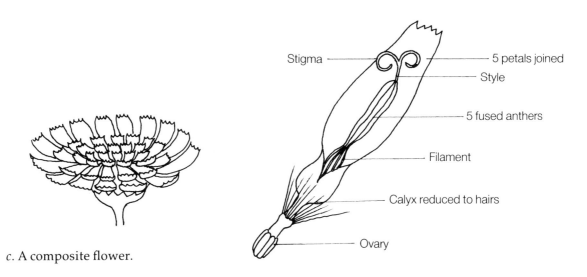

c. A composite flower.

d. Single dandelion floret.

Heliopsis – a composite flower.

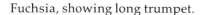

field garlic (*Allium oleraceum*) or African lily (*Agapanthus africanus*). A *corymb* is a raceme which has a flat or flattish top, like yarrow.

The line illustrations overleaf show some other flower shapes. The pendulous head of the fuchsia with its upturned petals and contrasting skirt presents a strong contrast to the simple open single flower of the dog rose (*Rosa canina*). The orchid flower is of irregular shape and is complex compared with the daisy flower of *Anthemis cupaniana*. The robust trumpet of the daffodil (*Narcissus*) contrasts with the dainty, bell-shaped heads of the bellflower (*Campanula*) and the English bluebell (*Hyacinthoides non-scripta*).

The colour illustrations show different flowers: the heliopsis, a yellow daisy, radiates its petals from a complex centre. The primula

Fuchsia, showing long trumpet.

Another flower shape with a number of florets growing to form one flowerhead. This delicate flower lends itself to detailed treatment. Fine brushes were used for all the paintings to create subtle colour changes and intricate design.

Honeysuckle
Lonicera

Judith Milne.

43

FLOWERS

Dog rose *Rosa canina*

Daisy
Anthemis cupaniana

Bellflower *Campanula*

Daffodil *Narcissus*

Fuchsia

English bluebell
Hyacinthoides non-scripta

Orchid
Orchis

Various flower shapes.

The bell-shaped flower of the azalea.

Note the rich depth of colour of the primula.

is simpler in shape and has a particularly rich, velvety centre. The trumpet of the azalea is a showy flower with its speckles of cerise adorning the inside of the trumpet. The tube-like variety of fuchsia is pendulous in habit.

You only have to look in your own garden or park to find a huge choice of subjects, which vary with the altering seasons. The spring bulbs are always a joy, the awakening of a new year, after a dull grey winter. The delicate blossoms of the late spring give a haze of colour to the trees and hedgerows. Then, in summer, we have herbaceous plants and spectacular roses which require vivid pinks, oranges and purples, and as we progress into autumn the leaves and berries bring earthier tones to our palette.

Don't forget wild flowers either. They are a very important source of inspiration, but it is essential to protect endangered species. There is nothing more beautiful than seeing a tangled blue carpet of English bluebells in a spring wood, or a field of buttercups thrusting their shiny golden heads towards the sun.

As a flower painter, I am eternally grateful for the tremendous source of inspiration and material which surrounds me. Each flower presents a new challenge and different artistic satisfaction. Remember all the different places you can visit for inspiration – parks, gardens, arboreta, plant nurseries, botanical gardens, country fields and woods, and of course your own back garden or even a window box. The choice is yours!

CHAPTER SIX

LEAVES, STEMS AND FRUITS

BOTANICAL INFORMATION

A leaf is made up of a thin, flat green blade, or lamina, of soft tissue, supported by a strong network of veins. Most leaves are joined to the stem by a stalk, or petiole, which continues into its main vein. A channel from the stem runs through the main vein to the network of veins in the leaf, to carry water and nutrients to the leaf tissue.

Leaves are the food-making organs of the plant, and their flat surfaces spread out facing the sun and light for nourishment. The shape or outline of individual leaves can vary within a plant, differences occurring from the top to the bottom of a stem. Leaves with more rounded ends give way to narrower, sharply pointed ones; and narrow and slender leaves become more bulbous towards the petiole or the leaf tip.

The basic shape of the leaf can vary enormously. There is the basic oval, a revolute, where the edge of the leaf curls under itself; a sinuate, or wavy-edged leaf; a lobed leaf like the oak; and a serrate, which is like a rose leaf (some leaves which have large divisions can be described as double serrate).

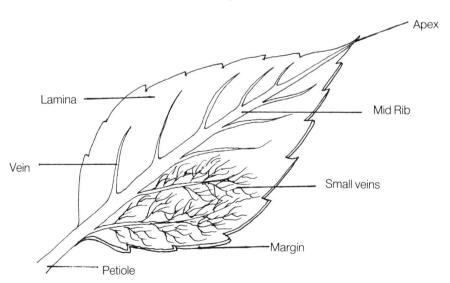

The parts of a leaf.

The veining system of a leaf gives it its surface pattern. In some cases the veins are pale and transparent, whereas in others they are thick and fleshy. The main vein on the upper surface is always obvious, but the smaller branch veins are not always apparent. In the case of the iris and gladioli the veins run parallel. It is important to look for the veining system; for instance, branches off the main vein may alternate, or may come from the mid-rib at the same position. If the veins are obvious, they should be included in the painting. Study carefully the pattern they form. Since the surface texture of the leaf is partly determined by the veining pattern, in some cases this affects the relief of the leaf: take, for example, the primula, which has an obviously complex veining system which gives the leaf its rugged surface.

In most cases the vein structure is particularly obvious on the underside of the leaf, showing quite a different pattern and colour from that of the upper leaf. For example, in some African violets (*Saint paulia*) the underside is a pinky red, in contrast to the dark green top surface.

Take note of the leaf's texture: is it smooth and shiny in the case of the laurel and rhododendron, or silken, as in the lamb's ear (*Stachys lanata*), with its soft down coating, or prickly and hairy, as in the poppy (*Papaver rhoeas*)?

The simple leaf is the most common type, although it can vary in proportion and margin patterning. The maple (*Acer*) is an example of a palmate, with its points protruding like fingers on a hand; a pinnate is a compound leaf with leaflets placed on each side of the stem; and a digitate such as horse chestnut (*Aesculus*), as the name implies, has leaflets originating from a central point.

Look also for the leaf arrangement, the way leaves are dispersed along the stem. In some cases they are arranged in pairs alternately, or at right angles to the stem, or alternately spiralling around the stem. A whorled formation happens where there is a circlet of leaves at intervals round the stem.

The habit the plant follows – that is, the way its stems and leaves emerge from the ground – is important to capture. Some plants are of trailing habit, whereas others stand erect. It is wise to portray your image true to its habit, so your composition will be dictated by the growth pattern of the plant you are painting. Stems may not seem as attractive as the rest of the plant, but will nevertheless be distinctive, so do not attach any less importance to them. Some may be smooth and shiny, while others will have a downy appearance. The faceted, square-sided stem of a deadnettle (*Lamium*) is quite different from the ridged stem of cow parsley or Queen Anne's lace (*Anthriscus sylvestris*). The fine hairs of one plant can contrast with the stronger bristly hairs of another, and thorns and prickles will vary in number, size and density. You may find that a stem is not

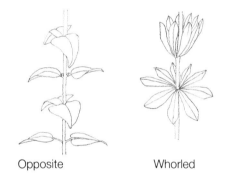

Opposite   Whorled

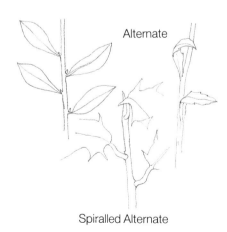

Alternate

Spiralled Alternate

Different leaf formations.

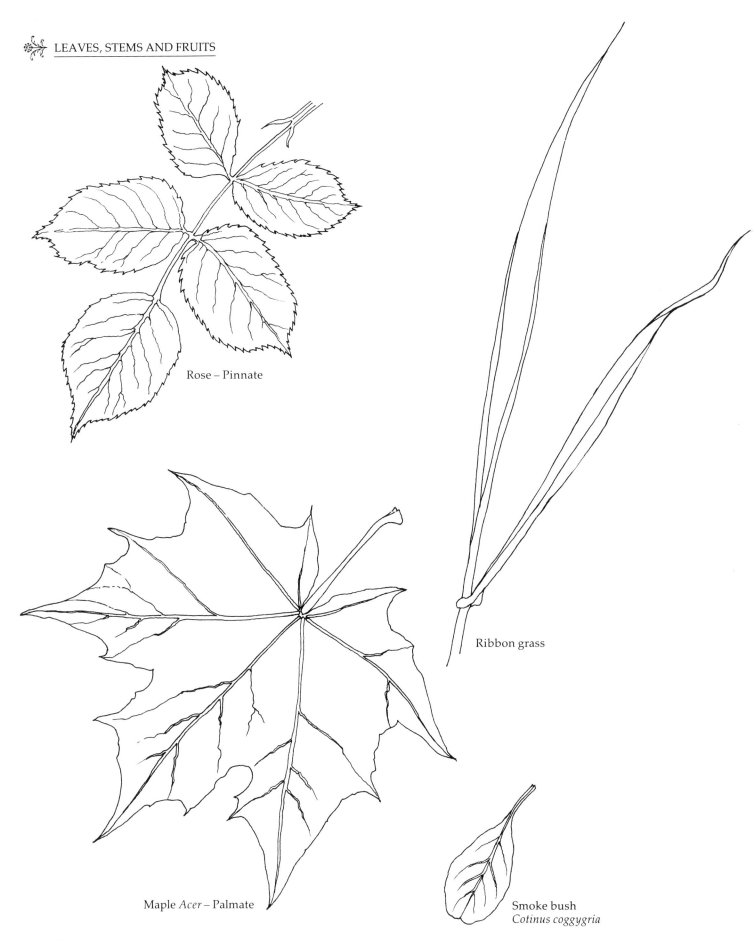

Rose – Pinnate

Ribbon grass

Maple *Acer* – Palmate

Smoke bush
Cotinus coggygria

Different leaf shapes.

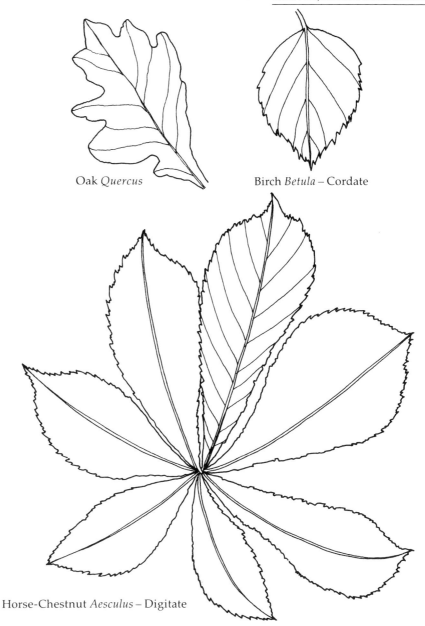

Oak *Quercus*

Birch *Betula* – Cordate

Horse-Chestnut *Aesculus* – Digitate

totally covered with hairs or thorns, but only in the area where it needs protection, so once again watch closely for those individual features (see overleaf).

Some of the more woody plants, such as rhododendron or camellia, have bark-covered stems, the patterns of which vary within the species. Leaf scars give specific patterning also, and with the patterning of the bark, these can help to create the distinctive shape of the stem and its three-dimensional effect.

Buds, like the flowers they develop into, have their own particular form. It is a good idea to include a bud in your painting, as not only does it add interest, but it shows a stage in the plant's growth. Sometimes it is possible to include several at different stages. Each flower species will unfurl its petals in different ways.

Stems. Note the different shapes
and textures.

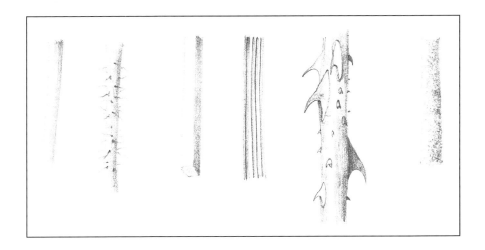

Fruits, also, have their own shape and character. Each plant will
produce its fruit following flowering, so you cannot study these in
conjunction with the flowers. In pure botanical studies, fruits and
seeds are never shown as part of the flowering plant, as in nature
this does not occur. Fruits vary from the brightly-coloured, fleshy
raspberry and strawberry, to the hips and haws of the hedgerows,
to the pods of the pea family, to the winged fruit of sycamore or the
nuts of the hazel and acorns of the oak. Each variety presents new
images to depict and problems to solve. Some will have a shiny
surface, others a rough texture. Observation is again the key. The
design of each seed box, which is what a fruit is, will be different
according to its method of containing seeds and ultimately dispers-
ing them.

PAINTING

One has only to glance at a garden to notice the endless variety of
greens in the foliage, and to realize that to master the art of mixing
those colours is a feat in itself. The brilliant yellow-green of a maple
may be silhouetted against a darker green conifer, in its turn next to
a pale blue-green fir – all the colours altering with the play of light.
As the seasons change, colour deepens and the rich golden yellow-
browns, russets and reds mingle with greens and evergreens,
giving a warm glow to the countryside. The ability to understand
those differences in colour is crucial when it comes to painting
leaves. I cannot stress strongly enough the need to experiment with
mixing in order to obtain the correct colour green for your painting.
You will also need to take the texture into account.

LEAVES

The following examples show a variety of different leaves.

GLADIOLUS

The spear-like stem of the gladiolus, like the iris and montbretia (*Crocosmia*), has a main rib and surface veining. For the palest colour, I mixed a small amount of Permanent Yellow and Sap Green, and flooded the area of the leaf entirely. Adding to this some French Ultramarine, I proceeded to work into the leaf, leaving the paler veins in the light colour. The play of light alters the intensity of green, so some veins are not as obvious as others, and in other places the colour is deeper, especially where shadows are dark. Here I added Payne's Grey to give that depth, especially along the main vein. A pinkish tinge to the vein and the edge of the leaf was flooded into the first layer of paint as was the yellow-brown of the apex. Finally, I used a dry brush to deepen the hollows between veins.

AFRICAN VIOLET

The African violet (*Saint paulia*) leaf opens up quite different challenges. The convoluted, rounded surface is slightly rough and hairy too. Owing to its shape, highlights are in evidence, but they need a mere hint of the palest green – Sap with a touch of Ultramarine. Laying this wash first, then blotting dry, I worked the next darker shade, blending the new colour into the damp colour to give a lumpy effect. Again, before the paint dried, I darkened the colour with more Ultramarine and a touch of Payne's Grey, this time using the point of the brush for a stipple effect, simulating the rough area. The fleshy stem is a pinky colour, which deepens as it nears the leaf and along its shaded side. This, like the leaf, is covered in hairs, but they can only be seen where the light catches them. Students often make the mistake, knowing that a leaf is covered by hairs, of putting in every one. To indicate the hairs on leaf and stem I used some Chinese White on a very fine brush (No.00000).

HOLLY

The holly (*Ilex*) leaf is quite dramatic with its deep colour, unusual spiky shape and lustre. The central vein is pronounced but the

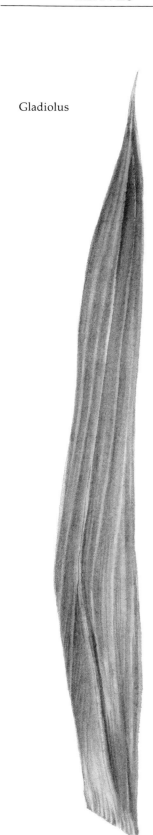

Gladiolus

African violet *Saint paulia*

Holly *Ilex*

lateral veins are shown by contour rather than by definition. The shiny surface means that the highlights, are very marked. I washed a pale blue-green over the leaf, leaving areas free of paint for the highlights, having decided to make the main vein a bright green, blending to an olive on the petiole. The shiny surface gives a mottled impression, so to convey this I used a stipple effect in the area around the highlight, deepening the colour with Payne's Grey. Towards the apex, the leaf curves away and falls into deep shadow, as do other areas towards the spikes. Looking closely, I noticed the leaf has a fine edge of pale green, which I added, touching the tips of the spikes with brown. The leaf is quite leathery and thick, and shadow could be seen along one edge, so with a fine brush I painted a thin line along the shadow line. The same colour was used to add shadow to the leaf stalk.

LAMB'S EARS

Stachys lanata, more commonly known as lamb's ears, is a hairy-leaved plant, very soft and downy to the touch. To create this surface meant giving the impression of tufty grass or hair, as the thickness of the hair parted in tufts across the whole leaf. The pale green stalk leads into the main rib, but is then diffused with the hairs, so no other veins are evident, only the hollow along the centre. The leaf is the colour of a pale grey-green; I mixed Payne's Grey and a minute touch of Permanent Yellow with a lot of water to obtain the first wash. The silken hairs give a sheen to the curved edge of the leaf, darkening the curve, then becoming lighter and then darker again along the centre. I laid small brush strokes of colour in varying tones to give the impression of the hairs, and over the lightest areas along each side. For the darker ridges of colour on the stalk I used a mixture of Sap Green and Olive Green. I worked the hairy fringe along both sides of the stem in the grey-green of the first wash, with short, fine brush strokes.

Lamb's ears
Stachys lanata

PRIMULA

The rugged surface of primula leaves under magnification is rather like an aerial view of the Alps, the veins forming river valleys in a fine mesh pattern. The first wash used was a very pale mixture of French Ultramarine and Permanent Yellow, giving a very soft shade. The stem had a pinky tinge, which I merged in before the first wash had dried, and strengthened where necessary. As the veining system is very complex, but more pronounced around the main vein area, I drew it first and then painted round the pencil lines. The patterning also varies from leaf to leaf, so treat each leaf separately. For the second layer of colour I added Sap Green, leaving areas free of colour to show highlight. I gradually deepened the main colour with more French Ultramarine and some Payne's

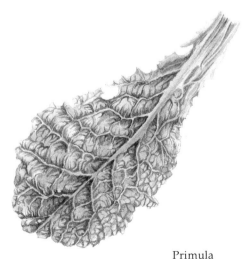

Primula

Grey to give the darkest tones. Where the edge of the leaf appears like headlands jutting into the sea, the veining is very close, and the surface uneven. Also look out for the darkest tones, which are around the central vein, as they will need to be accentuated.

Smoke bush *Cotinus coggygria*

SMOKE BUSH

The tiny autumn leaf of *Cotinus coggygria* presents a different range of colours. The veining is a light red, but there are deeper tones of red, yellow-orange and green. To get the perfect blend, work quickly, keeping the colour damp, so that it blends evenly. I added all these colours to the initial colour, avoiding the area of the veins. Scarlet Alizarin and Alizarin Crimson were used to varying degrees, with touches of Permanent and Cadmium Yellow, and Deep and Sap Green. Alizarin Crimson was right for the deepest areas around the veins, and a dry brush produced the mottled area on one side of the leaf.

CAMELLIA

I have already discussed painting a thick, shiny leaf, but the camellia is smoother, and its surface patterning is different. The same principle is used every time in starting your painting. The pale Sap Green colouring is a basic colour for the whole of this leaf; darken it with French Ultramarine and Payne's Grey. The plains are not as varied so the highlight is picked up down one side and patches on slightly raised areas near the main rib. The stippled effect is needed in this leaf, and in places I used Chinese White to give a stronger highlight.

Camellia

HERRINGBONE PLANT, PRAYER PLANT (see overleaf)

The raised red veins of *maranta leuconeura* show contrast with the variety of greens. I carefully drew the shape and vein system, then painted the veins in a mixture of Permanent Rose and Alizarin Crimson. Note, however, that the main rib is not all the same colour, so I left some gaps in the first overall wash of Sap Green and French Ultramarine. The veins stand proud of the leaf, so forming a ridge. Deepening the first wash mixture, I proceeded to paint the wells on either side of the main vein, leaving spaces for the lighter colour to filter through, and adding a little Burnt Sienna in places to give a sage-green colour. The strong patterning was a mixture of Sap Green, French Ultramarine and some Payne's Grey. I carefully followed the shapes before me, fading the dark area into a mid-green on the outer edge of the leaf. Again, I used a dry brush to give a slightly mottled effect, and deepened the tone in the hollowed areas between the veins. Then I applied Alizarin Crimson to the shadow side for each of the veins. Note how deep the shading is on the leaf stalk as it disappears into the leaf and how the green is olive

Herringbone plant, Prayer plant
Maranta leuconeura

in hue. The ridge down the centre of the stem is accentuated by the line of colour down its length showing shadow.

IVY

The last leaf example is the ivy (*Hedera*). This attractive plant, on close examination, can be seen to contain many shades of green. For the picture shown here I mixed a variety of greens, as I needed to flood one colour into another to get a soft and natural effect, with the paper remaining damp. Mixing a little Naples Yellow and Permanent Yellow, I quickly worked over the surface, applying to that the pale blue-green then the darker shades. All the while I checked the colour patterns of the leaf. In working damp, it is easier to get the variety of diffused colour without hard edges. When the picture was dry, I used a fine brush to line in the shadows along the veins. The dark red of the stem is a strong contrast to the lighter leaf.

Ivy
Hedera

FRUITS AND BERRIES

Berries and fruits.

These are a necessary part of a pure botanical painting, but perhaps a subject you may at first overlook. However, as the winter approaches and there are fewer flowers available in the garden, these berries and seed boxes can be another source for painting.

There are no hard and fast rules attached to painting fruits and berries. Just carefully observe their shape and colour. One fruit will vary in colour from that of its neighbour, owing to light and shade. Look closely at the cotoneaster and see the many colours in each berry, and how the highlight alters in shape on each side. The variety of reds and pinks on this bunch of berries is no exaggeration of how it actually appeared! I used the palest shade of pink first, omitting highlights, and gradually adding more Alizarin Crimson and Payne's Grey to get the depth of shadow. In places, Scarlet Alizarin was ideal where the shade varied, and in other areas a touch of Van Dyke Brown suitably deadened the colour. Note, however, that the highlight does not occur on the same part of the berry in each case, but is dependent on its angle and shape. Where a group of berries are close together, the shadow is a very deep tone. Stippling is a good means of showing the gradation of colour on the tonal scale.

The highlights of the rose hip were not as marked as those on the other berries. Cadmium Yellow, Deep and Cadmium Orange were first applied, and some Carmine added while the paint was still wet. Then with a damp brush, I removed the excess paint from the highlighted areas, drying it on a tissue, before lifting more paint until satisfied. Keeping the remaining area damp, I added the Raw Umber to give the tonal effect around the bulbous area, and the darker circling of the stem. On a round object depth of tone is patchy. The green of the sepals, Sap Green with Ochre, was blended into the soft yellow at the top of the hip and down the stem. The curved convex sepals were deeply shadowed on the inside and on the curved base. I added brownish tips and dusting on the other side with a dry brush, which also gave the fine serrations on the edges. Olive Green shadows on the stalk were added to the damp first coat to produce a natural fusion of colours. Note that the shadow is not just confined to the edge of the stem, but to the whole stem where the bulbous hip casts a shadow.

I hope my descriptions of individual plant components will now inspire you to attempt the whole plant. I have tried to convey the most important factors, but it is only a small cross-section. As you become more adventurous you will discover more complex problems, but experience can then be your guide to developing more advanced skills.

CHAPTER SEVEN

PAINTING IN DETAIL

When we paint, we have to make a personal decision as to how we want our image to look: detailed or free, impressionistic or representational. If detailed, can we get all the information from our subject matter, or should we look for a better specimen? These decisions influence the final result.

Some people have their own style from the outset, an innate talent, and if this is you, stay with it and build on it. On the other hand, style has to be developed, and that comes after a period of trial and error until the approach you find happiest working in is achieved consistently and is a part of you. To achieve success, always be ready to learn and adapt. So often, painting students slavishly imitate their tutor, and so end with replicas of the tutor's work. It is important to learn from many sources; combine the advice that sounds most sensible and create a style that is yours.

CHINESE LANTERN

I have purposely left this painting of *Physalis* unfinished to show all aspects and stages of work within one image. The vibrant orange colour of the lanterns demanded my attention, so I set out to draw the plant, having first found the best angle from which to approach it. I wanted to show the lanterns off to advantage, so eased them to face me centrally, whilst ensuring that the leaves still retained a natural droop.

Initially I made pale pencil lines, giving the directions and angles of stem, leaves and lanterns, then began to draw the outline (see overleaf). I used the angle of the stem as the key, then drew in the lanterns and leaves, with a clean outline. (I used an HB pencil on Arches HP paper, as I wanted a clear image for this first stage.) The natural position of the plant made a very satisfactory composition. Each lantern shape varied slightly, so had to be individually studied for shape, structure and angle. As I drew the stem, I also indicated the position of each leaf joint. However, I also exercised some artistic licence: two of the leaves sprouted from each joint to

All stages of painting.

Chinese lantern
Physalis

Plant positioned in oasis (*above*).

Pencil outline (*right*).

the growing point ending in a mass of growth, so I decided to simplify this by omitting some of these. On the leaves themselves, I only sketched in the main vein as I wanted to indicate subsidiary veins at a later stage, after the first, palest wash had been laid.

Having completed my outline drawing, I worked out my colour combinations. The nearest match was a mixture of Cadmium Orange and Scarlet Lake. With a No. 4 brush I applied the first layer of paint, carefully leaving highlighted areas free of any colour (it is always better to leave more of these if uncertain, as they can be filled in later).

As I worked, I tried to vary the colours as light and shade dictated. You may find this leads to colour variance with individual petals and leaves, but it can be adjusted as you work. Always try to sum up the 'tonal situation' in the first stage, as it immediately gives the painting life. I worked each of the three lanterns to the first stage, then left the lower one to concentrate on the two top ones. I checked the colour, defining some of the ridges, and suggesting the mottled appearance of its rough-textured surface, which has a number of superficial veins. The mottled effect was obtained by stippling with the point of the brush.

As I had left all the ribs highlighted, I realized that light only showed on two, so I worked a thin film of colour over the ribs, deepening the shadows and giving depth. The addition of Alizarin Crimson and some Payne's Grey to the orange colour slowly reduced the tone. At this stage I used a No. 1 brush for the surface texture and a No. 000 for veining. Finally, I concentrated my efforts on the top lantern, working it to completion. This one is viewed from a different angle, and it is possible to see the deep centre where the stalk joins the fruit. The dark shadows in this area accentuate the depth, with the ribs coming proud from the centre

Close up of a leaf.

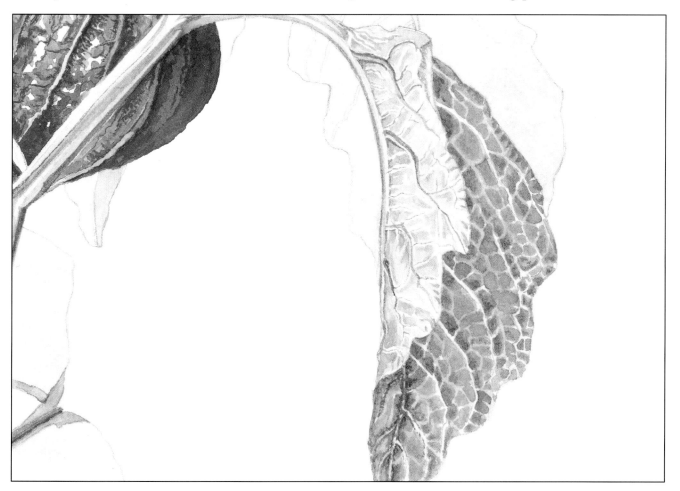

point. The strong pattern of the ribs and the rough surface is indicated by small brush strokes – think of the patterns as small plains, falling in different directions and catching the light. Here the darkest shades were arrived at by adding Alizarin Crimson, a touch of Van Dyke Brown and French Ultramarine. Some shadowed areas were a wash of colour, too dark to define pattern.

The stem is faceted so that where full light falls on it, the colour is very pale – a very watery mixture of Sap Green, French Ultramarine and Lemon Yellow. The darker area was a deeper mixture, and for the darkest side I added Van Dyke Brown and Payne's Grey. In places, the rib of the stalk has a reddish brown edge, and here I used a Brick Red. The leaf stalks have a very slight reddish tinge, the rounded underside being a pinky-green, whereas the flat top surface is definitely streaked with reddish brown. This effect can be obtained by painting the area green and, when virtually dry, using a dry brush to give the mottled red appearance.

The intricate detail of a painting of this kind is very time-consuming, so it is quite possible to spend one or two hours or more on each leaf. Owing to changes of light it is advisable to start only if you have a good length of time for working in the same kind of light. To complete a painting of this size, 38 × 28cm (15 × 11in) would take me two to three days.

The leaves were starting to change colour, and on close inspection, each leaf varied in colour considerably. The fresher top leaves were quite a bright green, but the lower ones were mottled patches of gold tinged with green. If your colours vary like this, decide on the lightest colour of each leaf, and then lay a film of this colour over the entire leaf.

For the yellow leaf I used Cadmium Yellow Light and a touch of Sap Green, whereas the other leaf was a mixture of French Ultramarine and Lemon Yellow. The upper side of the leaf was away from the light, but the light was showing through the veining, still giving a brightness to the leaf. I mixed Sap Green, Olive Green and Cadmium Yellow Light together to form the tissue shapes between the veins. The tissue shapes vary in colour too, like a patchwork quilt, and in places have a brown tinge, so I added Burnt Sienna. Around the veining, brown deposits formed almost outlining them. Once the whole tissue area was covered, it was obvious that some definition of veins was needed, so with a thin wash of colour I unified the area in each section. This also made the smaller veins less prominent.

The veins on the back of the leaf were a dark reddish brown and very soft, so I painted them in with a fine brush. Mixing Sap Green and Olive Green thinly, I worked between all main veins, leaving the base colour as highlight. In certain places I emphasized hollows with dark shading.

LANTANA

Lantana camara, a large shrub which originated in tropical parts of America, is often seen in Mediterranean resorts, with its multi-coloured globular flowerheads providing vivid colours. In Britain it can be found in tropical houses and conservatories. The florets vary in colour on the same head, changing from pale yellow, through orange to red, with cream and orange intermingled. The long narrow trumpet of each floret ends in an unusual, star-shaped petal.

This is an example of a delicate but complex flower, which you should attempt only when you have had some practice. Draw the head carefully, dovetailing all the florets into the outer given shape of the head. The colour within each petal changes from a deep central colour to a much paler hue on the outer edge. I used

Stage 1 – showing drawing, completed painted flowers at the top and a colour wash applied to the remaining flowerheads (*above*).

The finished painting (*right*).

Lantana camara

Swallowtail butterfly

Judith Milne.

Close up of leaf and flower.

Permanent Rose as the main pink colour, adding Naples Yellow to make peach, which could be deepened with a touch of Vermilion.

Each tiny flowerhead had to be individually painted, as adjacent heads vary in hue, and the petals have marked shadows on them. Because each floret was so small, I used a No. 1 brush and a magnifying glass to see the details.

The leaves of lantana have a rough, hairy appearance and the ridged stem is also hairy. I used Sap Green and French Ultramarine thinly as a basic colour, but before drying them completely, I added deeper tones to form the shadows. Payne's Grey darkened the green and was also applied with a very fine brush (No. 00) to define the ridges. Finally, I added the hairs with a No. 0000 brush, making sure they fell in the right direction.

I used the same mixture of colours for the leaves as for the stem, except where the light underside edges were showing. I worked the main fleshy areas between the veins, watching carefully for shadows, and the deeper area edging the veins. The fine surface veining was patterned with a fine brush and hairs added last of all.

When I had completed this, I then used a soft putty rubber to dab away gently any pencil guidelines.

CAMELLIA

I first made an accurate sketch of *Camellia* 'Donation' (see overleaf) ensuring that the flowerhead sat comfortably on its stem, and that petals radiated out from its centre point at the correct angle.

I then painted each stamen, using a pale cream colour, defining each filament and adding darker tones to give depth and shade (see overleaf). The anthers were worked in Ochre, with touches of Van Dyke Brown as shading. Another method of working a centre is to use a masking medium to cover all stamens – work petals then erase masking medium and finally work up stamens. This latter method may be easier, as it can be tricky painting around each detailed centre.

To work on the petals, I find it easier to deal with each one individually. I mixed up a weaker mixture of Permanent Rose, Permanent Red and Permanent Yellow. I covered the entire petal with this wash, but before it dried, I used a deeper shade to blend colour from the centre to the petal edge. On close examination, the petals shade out to a very delicate pink, which is a characteristic of *Camellia* 'Donation'. The next process is to add a small amount of Payne's Grey and French Ultramarine to your mixture for the shadow, working this into the centre and behind each preceding petal until you have the correct tonal value. Make sure you do not make these shadows too grey or purple, however. When you have completed the head, assess the tones, and strengthen in hollows to give depth. At this stage, I decided that the colour needed to be stronger, so I mixed more pink and laid an even wash over all the petals, so lifting the colour to the desired effect.

Another feature of *Camellia* 'Donation' is its deeper pink veining system. For this, use a No.00 brush and, in places, a No.1 rigger, but watch that you follow the natural line of the vein within the petal. Control the amount of paint you carry on your brush, by using a near-dry brush.

Camellia 'Dobrei'

Many shrubs have quite woody stems, so study the colour and texture closely. In this case, the upper part is a mixture of Yellow Ochre and Burnt Sienna. Leave some areas clear for the highlights. A touch of Van Dyke Brown deepens the colour of shadows. The junction of leaf stalk and stem are important areas to show growth, so look at them closely, if possible with a magnifying glass.

The leaf stalk is pale green and leads into the leaf as its main vein. As with petals, flood each leaf with palest green – a mixture of Sap Green and Olive Green, washing out the highlights to be paler still. Step-by-step, build up leaf colour to obtain the distinctive depths characteristic of camellias. Veining is not always visible, but where it is, work round the thin lines, leaving them as a tracery of background colour. Surface colour will vary within one leaf, so look closely for variance of colour. At this stage, veins can be *too* obtrusive, and so I tend to lay down a toned down wash to reduce their colour. Note that the underleaf colour and the reticulated edge of leaves are a different shade to the top surface. I usually add the brown tips of the serrations with a fine brush, but they must be blended to avoid looking tacked on!

Close up of camellia.

Camellia 'Donation'

The pink petals are very pale,
almost translucent, on their edges,
contrasting with the deep green
leaves.

ROSE

It was October when I picked this *Rosa* 'Prima Ballerina' (see overleaf for finished painting). I love the shape of a tightly-packed rose bud, and this one had such a rich velvety texture.

Using an HP paper and a F pencil, I lightly indicated the position of the plant on my paper. Once those directions were made, I then drew the detailed shape of the bud, followed by the stem and the leaves. Remember to indicate both the curl and the turn of the leaves, which gives them their characteristic shape. The starting point of the leaf is the central vein; if you follow its direction it will give you its natural curve. Once the shape is correctly drawn, then pay attention to the serration of the leaf. Draw each little indenta-

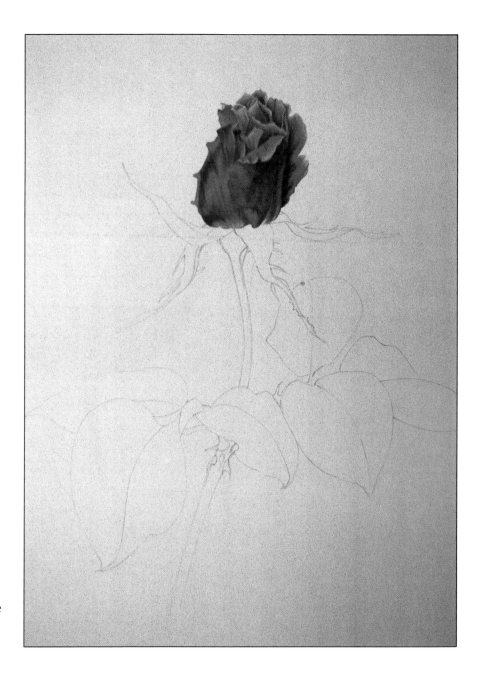

Finely detailed painted head of the rose, with the pencilled remainder of the plant ready to be painted.

tion except those that disappear if the leaf curls back on itself. Before painting, check that all the details are correct and that there are no superfluous pencil marks.

The colour I chose for the flowerhead was a mixture of Carmine and Permanent Rose, with some Prussian Blue to suggest deep, rich velvet shadows. Carmine is a strong colour, so a very watered down mixture was fine for the pale edge of the petals. A much deeper mixture of Carmine and Permanent Rose was flooded towards the centre, and I then added Prussian Blue for dark shadows. Initially, the lines were kept damp to blend the colour and to avoid hard shadow lines. However, to add some of the surface colour I used a dry brush. Treat each petal individually, setting one against another, so that the different tones create a three-dimensional effect. Watch also for the shadows on the bowl of the bud which with the light area will give the desired rounded appearance.

Having completed the bud, I proceeded to work on the sepals and stem (see overleaf). Roses often have a deep reddish-brown stem, which merges into green, and this flower was no exception. The seed box was bright green, so I painted this in Sap Green and a touch of Olive Green, adding French Ultramarine for shadows. Where the green of the seed box blends into the deep red stem I used Alizarin Crimson and Van Dyke Brown, with Payne's Grey added for the deep shadow on the right-hand side.

The sepals comprise a mixture of greens, from a very pale soft green on the inner side to a much deeper green on the outer side, to an olive green streaked with dark red. Hints of pink show on the inner surface of the sepal, and the delicate thorns are practically translucent.

The leaves face a variety of directions, so each plain is lit differently and must be treated individually. I decided on a very pale green – a mixture of Sap Green, Permanent Yellow and a touch of French Ultramarine. I then flooded this over all the leaves except for any highlighted areas, which needed to be left white. I then flooded more colour in, making sure that I washed the lightest colours first. I applied darker tonal areas too, blending them in before the colour dried.

Where leaves overlap, you get a very deep shadow, which throws up a top leaf and adds to the three-dimensional effect. In this example, the leaves were also mottled in places, and I depicted this effect by blending the colours whilst the paint was still wet. Notice, too, that the main vein area is usually the lightest, and that rose veins have a reddish tinge, as do the edge of the leaves to the point of each reticulation. I usually paint this tinge last with a very fine brush. Twirling the brush in my fingers against a cloth, tissue or edge of the paper helps to make the point as fine as possible, especially if the brush is beginning to wear.

Owing to the uneven surface of the rose leaves, some of the hollows fall into shadow. For these I used the same mixture of green, but added more French Ultramarine and some Payne's Grey. Occasionally when leaves fall closely together, it may be essential to emphasize some shadows or highlights to differentiate between leaves.

Rosa 'Prima Ballerina'

GLADIOLUS

Gladioli have striking, spear-like flowers and deep, rich hues. Here, I drew an accurate sketch of the plant first and then applied some colour. I used a combination of Permanent Rose, Vermilion and Naples Yellow; it was the inclusion of the latter that was the key to the correct colour, and gave me the softness of this hue.

Note the yellow tinge in the centre of the flowers and how the colour changes to a peach, and then becomes paler on the outer edge of the petal – almost translucent. The shade of the buds is a deep peach, which pales as the flowers become full-blown. This variety of colour within the range is obtained by using the same three colours, but using different permutations of colour strengths. The lower petals of each flower have a deeper centre, and the veins show up as Alizarin Crimson. Around the edge of the blown petals, groups of veins take on a mauve colour, adding irregular patterning

Flowers completed and leaves with first wash of colour.

Gladioli

to the petals. I used a fine brush for this effect, following the natural curve of the petal to suggest surface texture.

Anthers are a deep mauve-crimson colour, a combination of Alizarin Crimson and Violet Alizarin. The speckled appearance, where the yellow pollen encrusts them, is suggested first, before the background colour is applied.

Greens vary from pale green on stems and bracts to a much deeper green on the spear-like, ridge-veined leaves. The dark green gives a rich contrast to the delicate hue of the petals.

Peruvian lily *Alstroemeria*

AFRICAN VIOLET

I worked this painting of *Saint paulia* 'Harlequin' on HP 140lb (300 gsm) paper, a lovely smooth surface for detail.

The edge of each flower is frilled and is tinted with a pale magenta, which dilutes to white. To obtain the effect of the tinted edging, I washed each petal with clear water, and using a mixture of Violet Alizarin and Permanent Rose, I worked round the edge of each petal, allowing the colour to filter away from the edge. Some petals are marked with patches of colour emanating from the centre. In some places the veins are marked in pink. Payne's Grey with a hint of pink was the ideal colour for the shadow, and was deepened in places to accentuate certain plains. I used a very fine brush for the yellow stamens and pale pink stigma. A darker pink in places accentuated the frills, with additions of Alizarin Crimson and Van Dyke Brown for the flower stems and calyx.

Leaf stems vary in colour from a pale, almost transparent, pinky-green to a deep pink, which is also the colour of the underside of the leaves. While the pale green was still wet, I added the pink along the stem to create the diffused effect.

As with all *Saint paulias*, this one has fleshy leaves, with a slightly rough undulating surface texture. I used a pale bluey-green, Payne's Grey with a hint of Sap Green, and a very dark blue-green for the leaves. After applying the first layer, I kept the paint moist so that I could blend in shapes of darker colour without leaving harsh lines. The veins create the hollowed, dark areas, and in places I used stipple marks with a fine brush or dry brush on the damp paper to give the surface texture.

Close up of centre of painting showing flowers and their detailed centres.

Close up showing details on leaves.

It is advisable to assess leaf tones and ensure contrast is sufficient before using a fine, almost dry, brush to add the hairs in Chinese White body colour. These hairs covering the whole leaf surface are only visible when the light catches them, so you must only indicate those that are highlighted. The dull pink undersides of the leaves have pronounced veins, which you can show by working Payne's Grey with a slightly dry brush to form the shadows.

When completed, I removed all pencil marks with a putty rubber, touching up any remaining awkward spaces with a fine brush.

The finished painting.

African violet
Saint paulia 'Harlequin'

Flamingo flower
Anthurium scherzerianum

I used a brightly-coloured palette
for this exotic flower.

FLAMINGO FLOWER

The exotic, luxurious flowers of *Anthurium scherzerianum* have large waxy palettes, each with a coloured 'tail' at the centre. Although they are not an everyday choice as a subject, they do show a different type of flower and texture.

The highly glossy flower has deep 'wells' over its entire surface, with a variety of plains and tones. I used a mixture of Alizarin Crimson and Permanent Red to give me the basic watery colour wash, adding more pigment to the mixture to layer the colour, until sufficient depth was attained. Payne's Grey on its own would have made the shadows too purple, so only a little was used but I used proportionately more Van Dyke. It is apparent where the Payne's Grey was used; it shows a deep rich colour. Each hollow has a different shape which creates its own shadowed pattern. Not only does it have a hollowed surface, but it is also fluted, so the undulations have to be portrayed. I added the highlights last using Chinese White solid colour, with a dry brush giving the stippled effect.

The 'tail' is covered with nodules, forming a pattern spiralling regularly over the surface within a criss-cross design of diamond boxes. The counterchange method of light against dark and vice-versa can be seen as the tail lies across the flowerhead. The section of the underside shows the convex, bulbous surface.

Mock orange *Philadelphus*

RHODODENDRON

The choice of this variety of *Rhododendron* 'Winsome' exemplified several aspects of flower painting, all visible in the one specimen. Each flowerhead is seen at a different angle and varies in colour slightly; the leaves around the stem show both surfaces, and stems exemplify different textures.

The rich pink colour was a mixture of Permanent Rose with a touch of Permanent Yellow; this was thinly flooded over all the flowerheads in the lightest areas, with more pigment built up gradually for darker areas. The outer side of the trumpet was segmented by much deeper red lines, so I used Alizarin Crimson for both these and the inner trumpet markings. The rich tonal quality was achieved by adding Payne's Grey to the mixture, so delineating one petal from another, and emphasizing the variety of colour in each flower. Later, I used a dry brush to suggest areas of subtle colour change.

The flower stems are a soft salmon pink, merging into yellow-green, and to obtain this effect a wet-in-wet technique is best: the highlight emerges, as the shaded area is added before colour is totally dry. The fine hairs covering the stems are finally suggested with a No.00000 brush and Chinese White paint.

Close up of *Rhododendron* 'Winsome', showing the junction of the stalks and stem.

Rhododendron 'Winsome'

Judith Milne.

Note the many contrasts in texture.

Where the main flower stem emerges, I used a brownish paint merging to green for the coarse hairy area. I reserved the same colour mixture for the flower stem, only without the green.

The basic tonal area was worked before adding the green hairy texture. For this, I mixed Raw and Burnt Sienna, adding shade with Van Dyke Brown before the Sienna dried. The rough surface markings were created with a small brush and stipple effect to build up correct colour and pattern. Note the change of colour in the heel, showing the inside of the stem where the plant specimen was joined to the parent shrub.

Note the rough textured stem of this variety of rhododendron.

The narrow leaves have a slightly rough surface and undercurl. You can also see that the pink leaf stalk becomes a pronounced vein and changes from pink to green, and it is important to depict this point where the stalks join the main stem and show the growth pattern. For this I mixed Sap Green and Olive Green and painted a wash over all leaves, allowing the pink of the stems to filter. I added more pigment to build up colour around the veins, taking care to leave the highlights which ran along the curled edge of the leaf. Finally, adding Payne's Grey, I worked up the darkest areas, so silhouetting flowers and leaves. With a fine brush I touched up the definition round the veins and reduced their prominence with a thin wash of Olive Green.

The under-surfaces of the leaves are Olive Green with a pink fringe, so I used Permanent Rose and a touch of Alizarin Crimson for the vein. I then took away some of the colour with a clean wet brush, followed immediately with a dry brush to create highlights. With a No.000 brush I indicated the red veins, and strengthened the shadows with a mixture of Olive Green, French Ultramarine and Raw Umber. I worked along and in between the veins to obtain the curved effect, deepening the colour further to accentuate curves.

Carnation *Dianthus*

NARCISSUS

For this detailed painting of a narcissus, I chose an HP 140lb (300 gsm) paper, ideal for precise work. For many people painting white flowers on a white background is a daunting task, yet the problems aren't as great as you might imagine. Most white flowers do, in fact, have a hint of colour, whether it be yellow, green, pink or mauve.

First I drew the leaves and flowers to suggest their natural growth pattern, drawing a clean outline with an F pencil. (In this instance, the pencil outline may remain, unless you decide to run a colour wash behind the flowers.)

The deep golden trumpets that give these plants their jolly air must sit in the centre, with the petals radiating from under the cup. This shallow cup, with its frilled edge, gives a pleated impression, and Payne's Grey was added to the yellow to create shadows.

When you look at the petals closely, you can see that the clear veining and rugged surface form a pattern and therefore create the shadows. It is these you paint in varying degrees, leaving the remainder of the petal as the white paper. The colours I chose for the shadows were a combination of Yellow Ochre and Payne's Grey in varying depths of tone, giving the narcissus its characteristic undulations and form. Subtle use of counterchange – that is, light against dark and dark against light – provided the essential contrast and definition for light-coloured flowers against a light background.

Stems of narcissi are two half-circle sections, divided by a ridge on each side. The fact that they are often twisted also creates quite deep shadows. The lightest colour of the stems and leaves is a very pale bluey-green. The dark parts of the leaves are Payne's Grey, French Ultramarine and Sap Green. Further down, this deep colour gradually blends into a Sap Green, and like the stem becomes almost white where it joins the bulb.

The ridged veining is only obvious in places and heightened when in shadow. A steady hand and a fine brush are needed to make these lines in a dark tone. The ridges have shadows running along their length, and this effect is best obtained by using a near-dry brush to build up the necessary depth of colour.

The fine papery sheath that protects the bud and is so typical of narcissi presents a wonderful contrast to the fleshy stem. For this, lay a thin wash of Raw Sienna, omitting highlight areas, and before it is totally dry, add deeper tones of shadows where the sheath concertinas. Using a No.0 brush, paint in the fine veining, watching for its undulating pattern.

A good exercise in painting white
flowers.

Narcissus

Capturing the different stages of
growth on one stem.

Magnolia

Judith Milne.

MAGNOLIA

The waxy blooms of the magnolia are a majestic subject, but it is fairly tricky to paint a cut specimen as the flowers quickly fade. I chose a spray that had both a bud and a full-blown flower, and then began to draw the outline. I soon realized, however, that even the coolness of the room could not prevent the flower from fading, so instead of approaching the bud first, I set to work on the open bloom.

The rich magenta colour on the outside of the petals (Permanent Rose, Payne's Grey and Ultramarine) filters gently through the inner surface. I used a dry brush to create the fine mottling of pink around the deep pink veins and tinged some petals with Yellow Ochre and others with Burnt Sienna for a 'rust' look. In their natural habitat these blooms look predominantly white, but on close scrutiny the hollowed petals are heavily shadowed. The counterchange is obvious in this painting where the white edge of the petal is shown up by the shadows and the twists in the petals.

This particular specimen had died before I completed the painting of the head, so I used a flower from another twig to complete it. You may have to resort to such subterfuge too, so it is invaluable to have a good eye for detail in order to find a suitable replacement!

Close up showing detail of a magnolia flower.

Luckily the heat did not affect the bud as badly as the bloom, but nevertheless its shape had altered considerably by the time I had finished painting. The leaf buds are a soft green, a mixture of Olive Green and Lemon Yellow, tinged with Burnt Sienna, which I added with a dry brush. The bud at the bottom left-hand corner has deep Ochre-Brown covering with Raw Umber used as the inner shadow.

The woody twigs illustrated were quite an exciting challenge, their rough texture contrasting greatly with the flowing lines of the flowers. The upper stem is particularly shiny and differs in colour from the rough lower part. I applied a mixture of Burnt Sienna and Van Dyke Brown leaving a strip of white paper as the sheen. I then went over the 'sheen' with a partially clean brush to reduce the whiteness and make it less obvious. Stronger Van Dyke Brown was worked in to darken shadow and give roundness. The tiny buds were painted in Sage Green, and the speckled marks were created with a fine brush and Chinese White.

The lower part of the twig shows many small sections scarred with the marks of dropped buds. Van Dyke Brown was the foundation, but I used Raw Umber to darken and deepen the twig, with a touch of Payne's Grey. I left areas white to suggest both the scar lines and the highlights, and then slightly tinted those areas. Patches of Sage Green were finally added where lichen covered the twig.

The lines and ridges on this stem clearly indicate its shape and help to emphasize its structure. Therefore, it is important that you indicate the direction these lines follow in order to portray true perspective. Form can be lost totally if lines such as these are not accurately marked. With a fine brush I emphasized the ridges of these scars with a composition of Raw Umber and Payne's Grey and also deepened some areas of shadow. The cut end of the twig showed rings of colour, so I stippled my picture to suggest this fibrous texture.

Flowering quince
Chaenomeles

COWSLIP

I chose a hot-pressed paper with a very absorbent surface for the painting of *Primula veris* overleaf, which is more suitable for freer drawing. However, the paper does not stand up to over-use of an eraser, and I would have found my task of depicting the small, delicate heads much easier on a very smooth, firm surface.

Permanent Yellow was my choice for the petals, with a touch of Vermilion added while the paint was still wet for the centre; in the very middle the head of the stigma is visible as a pale green pin-head surrounded by shadows of a deep Olive Green with a touch of Payne's Grey. Slight shadowing is added to the petals to differentiate between them and also to show the cupping effect.

The narrow, pale green tube of the floret is ridged, and the calyx is segmented but joined to form a tube. The highlight is shown as a hint of green, whereas the darker green area is a mixture of Sap Green and French Ultramarine. Notice the variety of greens in this plant: the stems are a Pale Olive in colour with a little Van Dyke Brown for shading.

Leaves of all plants of the primula family (*Primulaceae*) are complicated and challenging. Draw them out carefully first, as the outer edge of each leaf will appear quite different in shape. Within the same plant some leaves will appear flat, while others seem much more curved with hollowed undersurfaces.

Cowslip leaves.

Judith Milne.

Cowslip
Primula veris

The highly textured leaves are the
main characteristic of primula.

Unless the highlight was particularly white, I mixed the lightest shade of green, Sap Green and French Ultramarine and covered each leaf with it. The highly textured surface makes for a contrast of shadows, and although the side veins are not visible on the surface, I indicated them with deep hollows on the reticulated surface. The shaded pattern area took a long time as I worked layer on layer of paint to create the desired effect. The central vein is broad at its base, and shows up light against the leaf tissue, but has a darker sage-green centre, sometimes tinged with pink. The greens vary considerably in shade within one leaf. As one leaf overshadows another, the shading takes on a deep bluey-green hue, which gives the image depth.

The slightly concave undersurfaces of the leaves show up the veining system, which stands out as a fleshy network. The hollows between each vein have to be worked up individually to obtain the concave appearance, while shadows fall along the veins accentuating their lines. The underside of the leaf is much lighter than its top surface, and the shadows have a leaning towards brown.

When painting a whole plant, as opposed to a section, check that all leaves link into their growing point. It can be confusing at the drawing stage, with lines going in all directions, to omit an important line, which only shows up when all areas have been painted. It may also be necessary to deepen shadows to emphasize the tonal quality.

Buttercup
Ranunculus acris

BIRD-OF-PARADISE FLOWER

I brought this unusual *Strelitzia* plant of South African origin back from a trip to Madeira, where it grows all year round, lasting for long periods even when cut, and sending out fresh orange blooms at intervals.

Its simple structure made it straightforward to draw, but I ran into problems trying to paint it in a heatwave! The subtle interchange of colours in the horizontal bract was problematic, as washes of colours, however liquid, dried instantly and created hard edges. My solution eventually was to keep the surface of the painting damp at all times with clear water, using a wet-in-wet technique to gently blend pinks, mauves, greens and browns. For the faint veining along the length, I used a dry brush as usual.

The flower provides a wealth of colours, with dull, earthy shades contrasting with brilliant orange-pink and indigo. Where the petals leave the sheath, a greenish pink changes to a deeper pink, pale orange and then finally to a deep orange. The other petals are indigo – a really inky shade – fading to mauve with just a hint of colour at the tip. The change of colour is subtle and needs to be run in when still wet.

Stage 1 – showing the drawing and initial painting of the sheath.

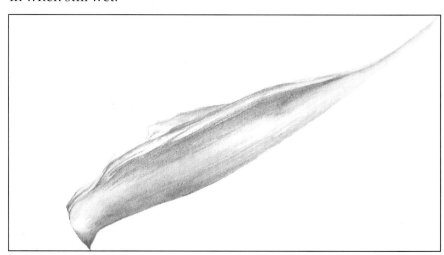

sheath and petals.

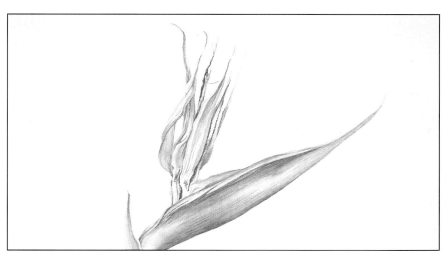

Bird-of-paradise flower
Strelitzia

Judith Milne.

The same wet-in-wet technique can be used for the stem, which
is similar to the iris. As you will see, the variations of greens are
subtle, and shadows deepen dramatically where each section emerges from a sheath. The vertical veining blends at times with the
background colour, but is worked with a No. 0 brush when slightly
dry. The edge of each sheath is trimmed with a lighter edging,
which is the basic shade first applied to the stems. It is toned down
where the stem is in shadow and the dried tips are painted with
Van Dyke Brown.

89

Christmas rose
Helleborus niger

CHRISTMAS ROSE

Helleborus niger, featured on so many festive cards, is a very attractive flower, and such a subtle colour.

This specimen was growing in a pot, so it was easy to paint it. However, I was selective about which parts I painted: as the leaves trailed untidily, I just chose some of the better ones. The flowers varied too, but in a more interesting fashion: some showed open buds and others were mature flowers, with their greenish hue. At a glance, the flowers appear white, but the outsides of all the petals have hints of colour, which range from yellow, peach, pink and green. Some of the shading is quite blue, but varies slightly from flower to flower depending on the colour in each one. Initially I painted the stamens and the forked stigma a pale yellow. In some places they are tinged with green or a darker yellow, and some in shadow are a deep ochre. Around the base of the stamens and the centre of the petal, I applied a rich Sap Green, which pales to yellow slightly before fanning out as the white petal. The deep shadows help to give the curve of the petal. A mixture of Sage and Sap Green

Close up detail of the heads of Christmas rose.

The speckled stems show clearly.

was used for the green petals, and a touch of pink was applied in places. I used a No. 000 brush for the veining in grey-green, making sure I let the lines follow the curve of the petals.

To get the smooth, gentle shading on the rounded stem, first flood stems with the lightest shade of green, a mixture of Olive with Sap Green. If stems dry, dampen with clear water, before flooding in deeper tonal shade on the shadow side. The shadow will blend with the lighter shade, so giving a rounded effect of the stem. The deep red markings on the stem are a mixture of a little Alizarin Crimson and Van Dyke Brown, almost dry. Make fleck marks with this, building up the right intensity of colour. If these flecks look too positive, blot them with a tissue, but remember that the flecks are deeper at the base.

The leaves on the right appear much darker, but are in fact in shadow. The lighter area of green, a mixture of Lemon Yellow with Sap Green, was painted first, but kept moist so that the darker green could be added and merged without hard edges. I worked around the veins, leaving them in a lighter shade, emphasizing them with a line of deeper tone. The leaves are fairly thick so it is possible to see their depth along the serrated edge, the points of which when dry should be tipped with Raw Umber. The main leaf stalk is ridged down its centre, forming a hollow. The spotted marks, as much a part of the plant as anything, are added last of all.

The undersurface of the leaves is much paler, and the veins stand proud of the surface; emphasize these with bluey-green shadows, deepening them until you achieve the right contrast.

AZALEA

The painting overleaf was worked from a section of a pot-grown azalea, which was a mass of showy flowers. I selected a suitable portion and drew a detailed outline of a side view and front view flower with leaves. I mixed up a watery solution of Vermilion and Permanent Rose, and covered the necessary area, omitting stamens, which look paler against the darker shade of the flower's centre. To create depth I put a thin film of Payne's Grey between the petals and on the outer side of the flower seen side-on.

In the second stage I needed to strengthen the pink inside the bell of the flower. The stamens are various shades: in one flower they are dark against the lighter pink, and in the second one they show up as pale against the crimson patterning of the three top petals.

Stage 1 – showing outline drawing and the first washes of pink, omitting the stamens.

Stage 2 – showing more details added to the petals; the painting of the stamens; and the first washes on the leaves, adding tone while the wash is still wet.

This patterning is created by using small brush strokes. The stamens on the left are painted with a mixture of Permanent Rose and Alizarin Crimson. The pink stigma broadens and this wider area falls into shadow under its top platform; the anthers are dark crimson. I began to indicate the veining in a slightly deeper pink and a very deep pink on the outside of the petals. I mixed Sap Green with French Ultramarine for the leaves, washing out areas with clear water to show highlight, and flooding in a darker green to give variation of tones. These leaves are small, smooth and glossy and it is useful at this stage to see tonal areas developing.

In the final painting the shading accentuates hollows and curves in petals and it is easy to see the slight fluting on the edge of the petals. The centres of the flowers are deeper in colour to give the hollowed effect, and the backs of the petals are dark, showing up the lighter edges of the front petals. Deepening tones along the anthers give them depth and prominence.

Some of the leaves show little detail except the main vein and some shading. For the rich dark green I mixed Payne's Grey to the original mixture of Sap Green and French Ultramarine. Notice how the deep shadows under the leaves throw the next one forward. The main vein is shown up by shading along its edge, and on the other side shading is built up by using a dry brush for gradation of colour and the mottled effect. Finally, I was not satisfied with the shade of pink of the flowers, so I placed a deeper wash over the entire area to give a more realistic colour.

Azalea

Completed image. The tone added to the petals gives them more depth. The details on the leaves show where light catches the shiny surface.

FUCHSIA

In this instance I began working with an F pencil on a delicate paper which I do not usually use, but it was adequate here as I was not applying broad washes. This particular specimen was just right, with plenty of colour variation and a selection of buds and blooms in different stages of development (see page 97).

The outer petals showed only a hint of pink, with slightly deeper veining, but the undersurface was slightly deeper with shadows accentuating the hollowed surface. For the 'skirt' petals, I used

Painted flowerheads. This is the important first stage.

Carmine and French Ultramarine, working carefully around the stamens, which were a lighter shade. The younger part of the stem and flower stalks was a bright pink – Permanent Rose was most suitable for them, and I toned it down with some Indigo. For the lower part of the stem I used green tinged with pink, working the colours while still wet so that they merged. The globular buds in stages of development vary between pale green and touches of pink; the segments show the forming petals.

The detail on the leaves is still to be completed.

The leaves, with a pronounced vein system, are bright green. I added Lemon Yellow to Sap Green to make the lightest shade, toning down with French Ultramarine to work the darker areas between the veins and along the main vein. The leaf margin is serrated and although it was not a thick leaf, slight tone is seen along its edge. I used a dry brush to obtain the darkest areas so that gradation of colour was subtle without having harsh lines.

Fuchsia

Judith Milne

The completed image.

CAMELLIA

I am very fond of camellias, and when looking round a garden centre to choose a plant for painting, I found *Camellia* 'Dobrei', which has such a deep rich, appealing colour. The plant stood about four feet high, with several beautiful blooms, so I needed to angle it in the best position before painting. Sometimes it is necessary to make small preparatory sketches to sort out the best position and possibly rearrange angles without losing character. Once this is ascertained you can then start drawing the plant on paper, making very faint marks. Remember to make a very detailed linear drawing, making sure proportions are correct before you paint.

As with most plants, I started with the flower, as that was unlikely to last in its best state for very long, although a freshly-opened camellia will last a number of days. I used a mixture of Permanent Rose and Vermilion, making it very dilute on the outer edges of the petals, where the light catches on the curves. The centre of the petals that forms a well is deeper in tone, and so Alizarin Crimson with a touch of Payne's Grey was most suitable. However, only add the Grey in moderation as it can make the colour too dark.

Close up of head and leaves.

Camellia 'Dobrei'

I found it exciting and challenging
to try to capture the rich colour of
this flower.

Judith Milne.

The paper that I used is a hot-pressed paper; its lovely smooth surface is ideal for fine, detailed work, but it can absorb paint quickly. To avoid hard edges, make sure that the paint is kept damp and moving, until the desired effect has been achieved. Colours will vary within each petal, so paint each one separately, carefully studying the colour change in each. The play of light on the different plains will also affect the colour and depth. To soften hard edges keep paint moist with clean water and dry it off with a tissue or a dry brush to get the required consistency. The fine veins on this plant were worked with a No.00 rigger brush (you could use No. 1) – the long thin flexible hairs give fine lines. I made sure that I followed the curve of the petal, so contributing suggestion of form, and used a slightly darker colour for the veins.

The stamens in the centre are a tangle of small fleshy stems which should be worked on individually, giving depth to the spaces between. Thin colour washes help to deepen the flower and a very small brush is needed to give the fine dusty appearance of the anthers.

Most camellia leaves are a rich dark green with a high-gloss surface, which creates strong highlights. Indicate these by leaving the paper free of paint when you apply your first wash. With most of the leaves, I started with the palest green, in this case a mixture of French Ultramarine, Permanent Yellow and a touch of Sap Green. Before the paint dried, I worked in a darker shade, carefully avoiding the veins and the highlighted areas. This process continues with darkening until the correct depth of colour is attained. Payne's Grey is a very good shade for deep shadow on the greens, particularly this shade. Pay great attention to the junction of leaf and stem or stem and branch, as this point shows the growth of the plant. Each leaf will appear slightly different to the next as the play of light will vary from one plain to another. The curl and twist of a leaf is a good feature to include, as not only does it show the naturalness of the plant, but also variety of shape.

The main stem is the feature you should finish with. This is quite a woody stem, and differs in texture from the stems of other camellia. Its outer surface is fibrous and where it is peeling you can see the paler tissues underneath. To obtain this texture, after using a mixture of Burnt Sienna, Ochre and Van Dyke Brown as a basic colour, I used a dry brush to get the hairy effect of the bark.

When you have come to the stage when you think your painting is completed, it is a good idea to leave it in a position where you can glance at it from time to time. Make sure it cannot be splashed, though, as that can ruin your work immediately. This quiet period of reassessment allows you to make slight adjustments, such as deepening the tone of a petal or leaf, until you are finally ready to store your work, or mount it.

CHAPTER EIGHT

PAINTING FREELY

Working freely is a very different style of art to precise botanical painting. There are no linear guidelines to follow, and your work is a direct statement, ungoverned by rules or precedent. However, it is essential to remain true to the plant, and portray identifiable characteristics. Basically, the approach is a simplified representation, observing all the salient factors but in a looser, more personal manner. Colour carries the same importance as in finer painting, but it may not be as easy to portray close gradation of colours to exemplify every variance that you would find in the specimen.

FULL-BLOWN ROSE

To begin a direct painting such as the one on page 103, it is just as important, if not more so, to study the specimen carefully as you will not have any pencil guidelines to help you; there is no way of overcoming any errors once brush strokes have been laid. I worked on a hot-pressed 140lb (300 gsm) paper, which was a good surface for working freely and with fluid colour.

I began, using a No. 000 brush, mixing Yellow Ochre with Permanent Yellow to make the dots of colour for the anthers, and the fine lines for the filaments. A little Van Dyke Brown varied the colour where some stamens were drying or shaded. When that area was dry, I mixed up Carmine and Permanent Rose with a No. 4 brush, both in the petal colour and its shadow tone, adding French Ultramarine. I had to decide on which petals to work, bearing in mind that adjacent petals will run into each other, so studied their shapes carefully. The petals were white at the centre, so there was no tricky painting around stamens. Working in this very direct way, I applied the light shade first, but added the tonal area before the first brush strokes dried. It helps to use a larger brush which carries more paint for this, but it is not possible to work on the petal abutting the one just painted, so plan to work on petals in different places round the flowerhead (left). Paint should not take too long to dry, but you can accelerate the process by using a hair dryer. The

Building up the head of the rose, petal by petal.

finished painting measures approximately 15 × 10cm (6 × 4in), so with warm conditions the paint dries fairly quickly.

Each layer of petals will be shown up by the patterns and shadows created by the layer below. These lower petals actually outline the shape of the upper petal. Work quickly, so that the darker shades blend in, and absorb excess paint to show the highlight with a clean damp brush, a dry brush or a tissue. Each petal will vary in form as well as colour – for example, the well of the petal is clearly defined and so it does not matter if it has a hard edge, but other petals with smoother shapes need more subtle treatment.

Additional colour, deepening your shades, can blend and diffuse into existing wet pigment with great impact. When painting in this fluid way, I avoid too many fine brush strokes, but leave the broad direct statement to give the necessary information.

My intention initially was just to paint the head of this flower, but I decided to complete the image by adding the stem and the leaves. Using Sap Green and French Ultramarine, and a No. 4 brush, I indicated the stems and leaves, quickly adding in the

Close up of head of the rose.

darker areas and vein patterns. The small thorns were added before the stem paint was dry, so that they blended, and the Van Dyke Brown was added last.

The finest part of the painting is the centre, but it still does not have the definition I would make in a more intricate study. This painting was worked in thirty minutes, but even so, the quality of colour and shape was just as important as if I were taking three or four hours to paint it.

Rose
Rosa

This full-blown rose was worked in half an hour.

Bearded iris
Iris pallida

BEARDED IRIS

You may think it strange to see this plant illustrated twice in one book (see also page 8), but it is very useful to compare a subject painted in both a detailed and a free manner.

Irises are not the easiest of plants to paint, purely because they wilt so quickly, and open at a rapid rate. Both paintings were carried out in excessive heat. If you are working in great detail, you will probably take a day or even two days to finish your painting, so you need plenty of flowers at different stages of development to use as a back up. With detailed painting, you have an outline to work to in your drawing and can match the shapes to succeeding specimens. Buds open rapidly, so it is probably advisable to tackle those first.

This specimen was top heavy, so I supported it in a weighted, narrow-necked vase to keep it upright and in a fixed position. The upper petals, which are more translucent than the lower ones, were painted with a mixture of Yellow Ochre and Permanent Yellow, thinly flooded to form the petal shapes. While the paint was still wet, I added the diluted dark red shade to the upper petals to give the variety its true mix of colour. Look carefully and you will see

Close up of bearded iris.

that these petals have a green vein running centrally through the petal; I added this after I had put down the petal colour, along with the additional veining, avoiding too many small brush strokes. For the rich, deep-coloured lower petals, I used a mixture of Alizarin Crimson, Van Dyke Brown and Payne's Grey. I applied this colour in its palest form to shape the lower petals. The yellow part of the leaves was kept moist so that the reddish brown would filter into it, so giving the blotchy effect, and then deep-coloured veins were added on top. Payne's Grey added to the Crimson provided a beautifully rich colour and the 'beard' painted with dots of Permanent Yellow was added after the main petal colour in a space left for it. A darker tone was added to give variation and for the hair-like support, standing erect like bustles.

The tightly-packed buds in the painting on page 8 are a very deep, reddish-brown. I worked in a touch of green wet-in-wet to blend naturally. The thin, papery sheaths, covering the buds, form virtually transparent coverings over the stems, which show through as deeper tones. Ochre tinged with green and brown was ideal for the stems, then worked in with a No. 1 brush to indicate the vein markings.

Leaves and stems are a vivid green. A wash of Sap Green was laid initially, then French Ultramarine added while the first colour was still wet, and a touch of Payne's Grey to provide appropriate depth. Although I did not include leaves in the free painting, I did portray one in this detailed study. The surface of these blade-like leaves is ridged, and so I used a No. 2 brush to paint in the vertical parallel veins. The ridged effect is accentuated by shading running along its length in deeper bluey-green. I also indicated a fine edging of translucent pale green tissue running along both edges of the leaf. This painting was worked to the size of the plant and is 30 × 38cm (12 × 15in).

Freesia

ENGLISH BLUEBELLS

A carpet of English bluebells (*Hyacinthoides non-scripta*) in a wood is the epitome of spring. When you look at them individually, it is hard to imagine them giving such a splash of colour, with their tiny delicate blooms. To paint this subject freely, consider every brush stroke carefully, as your statement once made cannot be altered. I applied a mixture of Cerulean Blue, Permanent Rose and French Ultramarine for the basic shape. Note that each petal of each bell has a ridge down the centre and a darker shade of their basic colour filters from this. Next, position all bells and their stalks before adding the stem; add filament bracts at the base of flower stalk, then the main stem; and finally leaves carefully worked around your pre-defined shape. This painting was worked in approximately 10–15 minutes, and whilst lacking the refinements of a detailed study, it does capture the character of the plant.

English bluebell
Hyacinthoides non-scripta

A ten-to-fifteen minute study.

Judith Milne.

TULIPS 1

These variegated tulips are so appealing, with their strongly contrasting coloured heads. I studied the shapes carefully, then applied a thin mixture of Vermilion and Permanent Rose, leaving the white areas as paper colour. I added Alizarin Crimson for the deeper shaded areas, mixed with Payne's Grey in places. The very definite shapes of the petals, with the central ridge, were then indicated by the veins. I let my brush follow this surface shape and it immediately conveyed the form.

As usual, I painted the flowerheads first, adding the stems and leaves afterwards. (Note that the shaded area of the under-petal forms the edge of the white petal and that brush strokes are much more obvious in this method of painting.) For the leaf and stem shapes I mixed Lemon Yellow and French Ultramarine, and before they were thoroughly dry, I added darker shades of the same colour, showing a curved area of leaves and shading the stems. Note the deeper shade where leaves leave the stem.

TULIPS 2

Overleaf I chose a group of tulips growing in a tub as my subject. The heads were painted in an even freer manner than the variegated ones, as the colour changes were more subtle. The Vermilion shade was blended with touches of Permanent Yellow while wet. For the middle flower I added Lemon Yellow with Vermilion before the paint was dry. The French Ultramarine was added to this one for shadow, whereas Alizarin Crimson and French Ultramarine were used to add tone to the others. All the painting was worked with a No. 5 brush, which was finely pointed enough for any lining.

I then added the leaves and stems after I had painted the flowers. Notice that I left the area where the leaf fell across the flower free of colour. Sap Green and Lemon Yellow were ideal for the leaf and stem colour and I darkened these with French Ultramarine where necessary. For the leaf on the left, I used superficial base colour to show the striated veined effect. I added shade and veining to the leaves on the right while still damp, and in some places I filtered in a touch of Vermilion to give authenticity to the colour, as in the lower stems.

Tulips 1
Tulipa

Judith Milne.

Tulips 2
Tulipa

Judith Milne.

RAMBLER ROSE (*multisign*)

This *Rosa* × *alba* 'Albertine' is a mass of blooms in my garden in June; its buds are a deep pink but change to a very delicate shade as each bloom matures. Although I painted this without any prior drawing, it shows more definition of detail than other examples in this chapter. I studied the shapes carefully before laying the first light pink washes. Permanent Yellow and Permanent Rose provided the slightly salmon pink hue and Raw Umber reduced the tonal value. Petals were worked individually to avoid merging and when these were dry a dilute mixture of Sap Green and French Ultramarine was applied to form the sepals. Before each dried, touches of Pink and Sage Green provided colour variation, the darkest areas being where the bowl of the petal sits on the seed box.

Rambler rose
Rosa × *alba* 'Albertine'

Judith Milne.

The twisted, natural shape of the stem gives more interest to the image, so do remember to look for the angles and direction it takes and put this across in your painting. Note too how the colours change down the entire length of the stem; if you keep the paint fluid the colours will blend without leaving hard lines where they meet. The seed box hidden behind the calyx is very dark, but the dark Sap Green changes to pink as it merges into the stem. To work this area I used a No. 2 brush with Sap Green, Alizarin Crimson and Van Dyke Brown in degrees, allowing spaces for the leaves and the junctions of stalk and stem. A No. 4 brush was used to form the basic leaf shapes, and I added in the darker paint to create the curves and vein patterns. More French Ultramarine deepened the very deep-bowled leaves and the shading on the bud. Leaf stalks and the serrated leaves were tipped with Alizarin Crimson with a No. 0 brush.

Before putting your painting away, check it against the specimen to make sure your tones are correct, and that you have not omitted little characteristic features such as thorns.

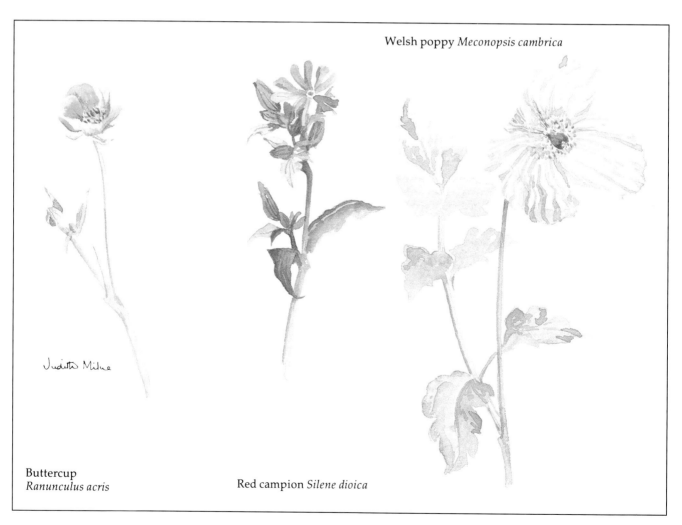

Welsh poppy *Meconopsis cambrica*

Buttercup
Ranunculus acris

Red campion *Silene dioica*

QUICK STUDIES

Rock rose
Helianthemum
'Raspberry
ripple'

Field poppy
Papaver rhoeas

All the examples shown here and on page 114 are paintings which were completed in 10–30 minutes; some were demonstrations to students, others were plant studies. They are all quite straightforward, and, though incomplete, they do capture the plants' characteristics. In each case they are worked to actual size – a process which becomes second nature after a while.

The buttercup (*Ranunculus acris*) clearly shows the cup-like head with the contrasting depth of colour giving it the immediate shape.

The red campion (*Silene dioica*) is a confusion of buds and the Welsh poppy (*Meconopsis cambrica*) has brilliant glossy, yellow petals with the distinctive creases done with Payne's Grey; the shorter lines on the top left show that the petal curves here.

The pretty rock rose (*Helianthemum* 'Raspberry Ripple') was painted with a No. 1 brush, which I used to mark in the Permanent Rose, leaving some areas white, then quickly adding Payne's Grey before the colour dried. The thin stems were painted in Lemon Yellow and French Ultramarine, darkened to shape the buds and leaves; I worked the shapes between stems to throw one in front of another to show depth.

The poppy (*Papaver rhoeas*) was a thirty minute study, appropriate as this flower barely lasts that time when picked, so it is essential to work quickly before the petals flop. The deeper Vermilion lines the petals to show the curves and hollows and the delicate green stems and feathery leaves below look hardly able to support the showy heads.

I used the pansy (*Viola wittrockiana*) overleaf for a colour demonstration of wet-in-wet techniques in one of my classes. The combination of Naples Yellow and Permanent Yellow was kept damp, and then reddish-brown was added to create the right colour effect for the petals. Alizarin Crimson, Van Dyke Brown and Payne's Grey gave the deep velvety colour required for the two main petals, and when I added them to the damp paint, it seeped into the background colour.

Apple blossom (overleaf) is a favourite subject as the blossoms are both cupped and white. By working the shadows tinged with pink veining, and using the green leaves as a backdrop, it is possible to shape your flowerhead. Note the contrasting greens of the upper and under surfaces of the leaves. The veins on both surfaces are worked in deeper tones of base colour, so showing vein pattern.

As for the rhododendron overleaf, I worked this very wet, blending the variety of pinks in the bell-shaped head. Touches of Payne's Grey indicated the inside, and the deeper coloured leaves defined the light side of the flower. Note the variety of greens within a leaf and how the deeper tones indicate hollows and curves on the leaf plains.

Apple blossom
Malus

Pansy
Viola wittrockiana

Judith Milne.

Rhododendron

CALIFORNIAN POPPY

Seeing a patch of *Eschscholzia californica* growing as a rich mass of colour in a friend's garden, I immediately wanted to paint it. It was not until I looked closely into the centre, that I realized just how deep the shade was – the stamens are the same pale orange as the outermost tip of the petals. I mixed Permanent Yellow with a dash of Permanent Red, and washed in the shape of one petal after another, varying the colour as necessary for each petal. I shaded the Vermilion centre evenly, making it lighter towards the outer edge of the petal, and where the colour dried, I dampened any harsh lines with clear water. Instead of drawing in the stamens, I worked in the negative, by using the shape of the darker colour to create the paler stamens against the deeper red of the petals. Shaded areas are Raw Umber, which added to the basic colour indicates slight fluting. The bud was painted using the same colours, but I added pink to the platform at the base of the petals.

The green of the stems and feathery leaves varies considerably, and so I used Permanent Yellow, Sap Green and French Ultramarine for some, and Lemon Yellow and French Ultramarine for others. You will see that the stems are a yellowish green, while the leaves in some instances have a blueish hue. To work this delicate

Close up of the head (see overleaf for finished painting).

Here I added the leaves, but not the shadows.

tracery, I used a No. 1 brush in direct lines, making sure I had ample paint on the brush to paint a length, keeping it moist to produce a continuous flow of colour. Darker shades formed shadows and indicated the ridged stems, and I paid special attention to the leaf and stem joints where the ridge patterns change.

I indicated leaf shapes by applying a flat area of colour, suggesting their haphazard curl and twist with a darker shade and simple brush strokes (left). Compare this with the final picture (below), and you will see how much difference this tonal shading makes to the fingers.

Californian Poppy
Eschscholzia californica

IRIS

Although this *Iris sibirica* is quite similar to the bearded iris (page 104), it is rather more delicate and its shape lends itself to an elongated composition. (It is always better to vary the shape of your compositions, and the very nature of your subject matter will usually dictate your choice.)

Here I worked to the same methods, painting the head first, adding petal to petal, but making sure I did not lose the overall

Iris
I. sibirica

shape. When working without any structural line, it is very easy to make the wrong mark and lose proportion totally, so constantly keep that in mind.

I used Naples Yellow for a creamy yellow, adding Violet Alizarin to merge the edges and work to the outer tips of the petals. In places there were hints of pink where I added Carmine for variation. I introduced French Ultramarine to Violet Alizarin for the shadow area, and also the veining, which is strongly marked. The sheath is a dark Burnt Sienna with some Van Dyke Brown added, made thin enough to allow the bud to show through. The Sap Green stems and leaves had a little Lemon Yellow added in places, then to darken I mixed in French Ultramarine.

Note how the ridged parallel veins are created with just a brush stroke, and how the edge of iris leaves are sometimes fluted in places. I used a No. 3 brush throughout, except for fine lines which were completed with a No. 0 brush.

HIBISCUS

The beautifully exotic flower opposite is so rich to paint, appearing in a variety of lovely colours. I painted the long branched stigma in pale Permanent Rose first.

Then for the underside of the petals I used a dilute Permanent Red. Each petal is a slightly different colour, where light falls on to the surfaces. Permanent Yellow added to one petal gave a more orange glow. I used Carmine and Alizarin Crimson for the inner curve of the petals, fanning the colours out as fine veins with a No. 00 brush. The deep velvety, cone-like centre colour was a mixture of Permanent Red, Alizarin Crimson and Payne's Grey; the same colour formed the shadows under each petal and on the cone, so making the curved protruding petal come forward. Using a No. 000 brush and Carmine I touched up the head of the stigma, darkening the edge to give shadow. The fine hair-like stamens were added and in places merge with the background; the filaments are a deep Yellow Ochre.

The calyx is composed of several layers of bright green structures for which I used a No. 3 brush and a mixture of Sap Green and Permanent Yellow with French Ultramarine for darker shades. These combinations of colours were used for stems and leaves throughout in varying degrees. I worked the area between the veins in a deeper shade, leaving the veins showing and then darkening a line along the vein to highlight them. The darker undersurface is a more bluey-green and helps to accentuate the curved leaf.

Hibiscus

ORCHID

The orchid (*Miltoniopsis* 'Eros') is pansy shaped, and can be found in a variety of colours. This painting was done on a Bockingford paper and worked in about twenty minutes. I quickly painted in the Cadmium Yellow deep centre, adding a little red patterning. I used a No. 5 brush to work in all the petal shapes in a watery mix of Carmine and Payne's Grey, immediately adding a deeper pigment. With a clean brush I absorbed excess paint in the area where the highlight showed. As the paint was drying I used the darkest tone to deepen the shadows, and create the hollow on one of the petals. Using a fine brush, I added the dots of colour that can be seen in the white patches and slight veining.

The simple leaves are a very light shade of green, slightly darkening on the edges, and deepening considerably along the central vein.

Orchid
Miltoniopsis 'Eros'

MARIGOLD

This study of a calendula was painted quickly in just twenty minutes. First the stamens – a simple stipple of Indian Red. Cadmium Orange, deep Cadmium Yellow and Permanent Yellow then shaped the petals with their toothed outer edges. The paralleled, ridged lines down the petals were worked with a No. 0 brush and Burnt Sienna, and in places where petals overlapped this was used as a shadow.

A mixture of French Ultramarine and Lemon Yellow was the base colour for all leaves and stems, but in places the colour was more yellow, so I used a little Permanent Yellow added while still wet. The ridged stem required darker, linear tones, and the curves on the wavy leaves were emphasized by darker patches of colour. The dark line running along the vein shows up the hollow.

Marigold
Calendula

BELLFLOWER

To paint freely, it is always more effective to keep your paint fluid. A combination of Cerulean Blue and Violet Alizarin created the true colour of this campanula. I worked quickly, painting in the lovely pointed petals, leaving spaces for the stamens, and working the spaces in between with a No. 5 brush. (Larger brushes are best for fast work as they hold more paint.) The pale mauve varies and is tinged with blue in places, yet in others a deeper purple has been worked in. A fine brush line drawn in along the centre of the petal merges in places with the petal colour.

The strong light contrast was suggested with the variance of greens. The stamens were painted in last, and I used Lemon Yellow, darkening the edges with Payne's Grey. The final finished effect is a loose, direct approach with a very fresh appeal.

Bellflower
Campanula

Judith Milne.

Narcissi in a vase (opposite; see overleaf for method). When painting a group of flowers, remember that the shapes formed between the flowerheads are just as important as the flowers themselves.

Judith Milne.

DAFFODILS AND NARCISSI IN A VASE

I first worked the vase, using Payne's Grey, but only working to the front lip, not the elipse. When I began, the daffodil trumpets were just buds, so I worked on the open narcissi, indicating the orange centres with Permanent Red and Permanent Yellow. I tinged the 'white' petals with a pale Naples Yellow, adding Payne's Grey when the first colour was dry.

Don't forget when working freely to look for the spaces in between shapes, as well as the shapes of the flowers and leaves themselves.

The next day, the daffodil trumpets had opened, so I worked the deeper yellow trumpets with Permanent Yellow, with some deep Permanent Yellow to strengthen the colour at the outer frill. Next I used a mixture of Permanent Yellow and Lemon Yellow for the petals, observing the shapes carefully before putting them down. Payne's Grey added to Yellow giving the right depth of tone and colour for the shadow areas. The green seed boxes and papery brown sheath were completed next and then the stems. I worked the leaves in very fluid paint, adding darker tones before the colour was fully dry, but in some cases where there was a very definite difference in tone, it was essential to let the paint dry first. In places I deepened the tone on stems and leaves to give the necessary contrast.

The background painting was worked freely and quickly to add interest. Note how the shadows on the wall help to show up the shape of the vase and give a counterchange of colour. This painting was worked on Bristol board, which has a very white, smooth surface, and allows the paint to lie on its surface, adding to the free effect. The surface of Bristol Board is usually better suited to small fine paintings. I used Nos. 2, 4 and 6 brushes.

CHAPTER NINE

FRAMING

You may think a chapter devoted to mounting and framing is unnecessary when your main concern is painting. However, you will come to a stage fairly quickly when you wish to frame a completed piece of work. The difference between a framed and unframed piece of work, however good or bad, is enormous, and apart from the personal satisfaction of seeing your picture smartly presented, framing is a useful means of protection.

If you are handy with tools, it is straightforward to cut both mounts and mouldings. Watercolours always need to be protected from the atmosphere, so have glass to set into the frame. A cardboard border or mount surrounding the painting improves the final appearance too.

Mounting board is readily available at art suppliers in a variety of thicknesses and colours, so if you are to mount it yourself, take your image along and choose a suitable colour. Consider the predominant colours in your painting or pick a complementary or contrasting colour.

Pre-cut mounts can also be bought in a variety of colours and in standard sizing; if you use them you will need to work your painting to fit these standard sizes. Mounts are more professional if cut with a bevel. You can do this yourself with a steady hand, and a sharp Stanley knife or a hand-held mount-cutter. If you want a really professional finish, go to a specialist mount-cutter in a framing shop.

The width of the mount is dependent on the size of the painting, but there are no set rules. In some cases it has become fashionable and effective to place a very small image in a large mount, so drawing the viewer's eye into the image. However, a good guide for the size of your mounts is to make the top and side margins the same width, and the bottom one slightly deeper.

I often embellish a single mount with coloured lines round the window. These can be of varying thickness or created with line

and wash – that is, lines drawn and filled in with a watercolour wash in a colour related to the image. These have to be executed very precisely and need a steady hand and eye. Always use a ruler and ruling pen filled with watercolour and a colour wash to fill in between the two lines. Alternatively, strips of marbling have become a popular choice instead of a wash. These come in a wide variety of colours, and are very attractive. The marble can be chosen to colour coordinate with the painting, and is easily applied to guidelines on the mount.

A double mount – a mount within a mount – is quite an impressive method of presentation, and does not always require the added decoration of line and wash (left). Using board of the same colour, or contrasting colours, cut the top mount about 1cm (⅜in) larger than the under one, so that the under one shows through it. It is possible to insert marbling strips on this under layer of board, or use the contrasting colour mount board for the under one, to give depth to the picture and colour link the mount with the painting. Different paintings demand varying treatments, so it is a good idea to enhance your work in as interesting a way as possible. In some instances, artists incorporate the mount into their design, by continuing their painting onto the mount. This can work satisfactorily and effectively but can be overdone, and make the image cluttered.

Besides the square/oblong cut mount, oval and round mounts are effective. Your subject matter will dictate the shape of your mount to a great extent, unless you design your image with the shape of the mount in mind. Either work to a definite mount size, or paint freely and afterwards tailor-make your mount to fit the painting. Incidentally, for a good result, round and oval mounts are best cut professionally.

A frame enhances a picture and glass protects it from damp and dust. A variety of mouldings are readily available for the artist who prefers to make his own frames, but a far greater number is available in a picture framers, where they have the skill and expertise to make a perfect job. Your choice of moulding should enhance the picture, and be of the right size and weight. A small delicate flower painting would look totally overpowered in a thick, heavy wooden frame, so it is a good idea to choose carefully, trying different frame samples against your painting, before making a decision. A professional framer will have many samples to show you in different colours and sizes, from the very plain simple frames to the more ornate, antique frames to the modern plain woods – gilts or painted. Once again the image you have created should influence your choice. The frame should complement it, and not detract your eye from your painting within it. It should be a total concept of painting, mount and frame.

INDEX

Actinodium Cunninghari 12
African violet (*Saint paulia*) 35, 47, 51, *51*
  'Harlequin' 72–3, *72, 73*
Agapanthus *13*
Apple blossom (*Malus*) 113, *114*
Azalea 45, *45,* 93–4, *93, 94*

Bauer, Ferdinand 12, 14
Bearded iris (*Iris pallida*) *7, 8, 9,* 105–6, *104, 105*
Bellflower (*Campanula*) *1, 44,* 122, *122*
Birch (*Betula*) 49
Bird-of-paradise flower (*Strelitzia*) 88–9, *88, 89*
Body colour 73, 75
Botanical Magazine, The 12
Brushes 19–20
Buds *7,* 49
Buttercup (*Ranunculus acris*) 87, *112,* 113

Californian poppy (*Eschscholzia californica*) 115–6, *115, 116*
Camellia 53, *53*
  'Dobrei' *63,* 98–100, *98, 99*
  'Donation' 63–4, *64, 65*
Cape leadwort (*Plumbago auriculata*) 25
Carnation (*Dianthus*) 79
Chinese lantern (*Physalis*) 56–60, *57, 58, 59*
Christmas rose (*Helleborus niger*) *90,* 91–2, *91, 92*
Colour charts 36, *38, 39*

Coloured inks 16
Colours and colour mixing 32–40
Composition 25–6
Counterchange 75, 80, 83, 124
Cow parsley (*Anthriscus sylvestris*) 27, 47
Cowslip (*Primula veris*) 85–7, *85, 86*
Curtis, William 12

Daffodil (*Narcissus*) 44, 80, *81,* 123, 124
Daisy (*Anthemis cupaniana*) *6,* 44
Dog rose (*Rosa canina*) 44
Drawing 23–31

Ehret, Georg Dionysius 10
English bluebell (*Hyacinthoides non-scripta*) 44, 107, *107*
Equipment 15–22, 23

Fitch, Walter Hood *13,* 14
Flamingo flower (*Anthurium scherzerianum*) 74, 75
Flowering quince (*Chaenomeles*) *84*
Flower structure 41–5
Foxglove (*Digitalis*) 41
Framing 125–6
Fruits and berries 50, 55, *55*
Fuchsia *43,* 44, 95–7, *95, 96, 97*

Gladiolus 51, *51,* 69–71, *69, 70*
Gouache 16

Heliopsis 43
Herringbone plant (*Maranta leuconeura*) 53–4, *54*

Hibiscus 118, *119*
  Syriacus 'Blue Bird' *34*
History of flower painting 10–14
Holly (*Ilex*) 51, *51*
Honesty (*Lunaria biennis*) 30, *30*
Honeysuckle (*Lonicera*) 43
Horse-Chestnut (*Aesculus*) 49

India rubber tree (*Ficus elastica*) 30, *30*
Iris (*Iris sibirica*) 117–8, *117*
Ivy (*Hedera*) 54, *54*

Lamb's ears (*Stachys lanata*) 47, 52, *52*
Lantana (*Lantana camara*) 61–2, *61, 62*
Leaf structure 46–9, 51–4
Leopard's bane (*Doronicum*) 24
Linear drawing 23–5, 26–8
Lupin (*Lupinus*) 41

Magnolia 83–4, *82, 83*
Maple (*Acer*) 48
Marigold (*Calendula*) 121, *121*
Masking medium 17
Materials 15–22
Michaelmas daisy (*Aster novi-belgii*) 31
Mock orange (*Philadelphus*) 75
Mounts 125–6

Narcissus *44,* 80, *81, 123,* 124

Oak (*Quercus*) 49
Orchid (*Orchis*) 44
  Miltoniopsis 'Eros' 120, *120*

127

Paints 15–16
Painting freely 101–24
Painting in detail 56–100
Pansy (*Viola wittrockiana*) 113, *114*
Paper 18–19
Pen and ink 17, 30
Pencils 17
Peruvian lily (*Alstroemeria*) *71*
Petunias *19*
Plant material 20–2
Poinsettia (*Euphorbia pulcherrima*) *32, 33*
Poppy (*Papaver rhoeas*) 47, 113, *113*
Preparatory studies 23–6
Primula 45, 52, *52*, 85–7, *85, 86*

Quick studies *112*, 113, *114*

Rambler rose (*Rosa × alba* 'Albertine') 111–12, *111*
Red campion (*Silene dioica*) *112*, 113
Redouté, Pierre Joseph *11*, 12
Rhododendron 113, *114*
'Winsome' 76–9, *76, 77, 78*
Ribbon grass *48*
Rock rose (*Helianthemum* 'Raspberry Ripple') 113, *113*
Rose (*Rosa*) 48
full-blown 101–3, *101, 102, 103*
'Prima Ballerina' 66–8, *66, 68*
Rose hip 30, *30*
Rubber plant (*Ficus elastica*) 30, *30*

Sketchbooks 23
Smoke bush (*Cotinus coggygria*) 48, 53, *53*
Stems 46–9, *50*

Tamarisk (*Tamarix*) *21*
Tone 28–30
Tulips (*Tulipa*) 108, *109, 110*

Water-soluble crayons 30
Welsh poppy (*Meconopsis cambrica*) *112*, 113
Wet-in-wet 76, 88, 89, 113
Wild flowers 45

Yellow wort (*Blackstonia perfoliata*) *25*